The Investor's Guide
to Technical Analysis

The Investor's Guide to Technical Analysis

C. COLBURN HARDY
Registered Investment Adviser

McGRAW-HILL BOOK COMPANY

New York   St. Louis   San Francisco   Auckland   Bogotá
Düsseldorf   Johannesburg   London   Madrid
Mexico   Montreal   New Delhi   Panama
Paris   São Paulo   Singapore
Sydney   Tokyo   Toronto

Library of Congress Cataloging in Publication Data

Hardy, C. Colburn.
  The investor's guide to technical analysis.

  Bibliography: p.
  Includes index.
  1. Investment analysis.   2.   Investments.
I. Title.
HG4521.H239   332.6'78   78-577
ISBN 0-07-026365-5

1234567890 BPBP 7654321098

*The editors for this book were W. Hodson Mogan and Janine Parson,
the designer was Naomi Auerbach, and the production supervisor
was Teresa F. Leaden. It was set in Electra
by University Graphics, Inc.*

Printed and bound by The Book Press.

Contents

Acknowledgments   ix
Disclaimer   xi

ONE   *How Technical Analysis Can Boost Stock Market Profits* ...   *1*

A Practical Tool   2
History of Technical Analysis   3
Technical versus Fundamental Analysis   3
Negatives of Technical Analysis   6
About This Guide   7

TWO   *Stock Market Theories and Their Use* *9*

Dow Theory   9
Elliot Wave Theory: For Long-Term Forecasting   17

THREE   *How to Plot Charts* *20*

Point and Figure Charts   21
Bar Charts   24

FOUR   *How to Read a Chart* *27*

FIVE *The Importance of Trendlines* *30*

What to Watch for in Trendlines 32
Long-Term Trends 34
Variations of Trendlines 34

SIX *Chart Patterns: Plain and Fancy* *36*

The Reliable V Formation 37
Tops and Bottoms 39
Head & Shoulders: More Fun Than Profit 42
Flat Patterns 44
Triangles Are Tricky 45
Flags and Pennants 48
Gaps Can Point to Profits 49
Don't Get Caught in a Trap 51
50% Rule 52
Unfavorable Patterns 53
Breakouts Are Always Important 54
Using Hindsight 57

SEVEN *Forecasting Indicators for Strategy and Tactics* *58*

Seasonal Forecasters 59
Best Times to Buy 61
Other Forecasting Tools 62
Short Interest: A Handy Predictor 66
London Stock Market Index 69

EIGHT *Channels, Support and Resistance Levels and Consolidation
Areas* *71*

Support and Resistance Levels 73
Consolidation Areas 77

NINE *Checking the Financial Pages* *79*

Most Active Stocks: What Major Investors Are Buying and Selling 79
Advance/Decline (A/D) Line 84
Highs and Lows 86

TEN *Moving Averages for Signals, Evaluation and Trading* *88*

Uses of the MA 89
Special 200-Day Moving Average Ratio 92

ELEVEN *Other Indicators: Good for Signals, Better for
Confirmation* *95*

Short-Term Trading Guide 95
Barron's Confidence Index 96

Signs of a Market Top   98
Speculation Indices   99
Special Indicators   99
Composite Index   101
Volume and Velocity   102

TWELVE   *Watch What the Federal Reserve Board Is Doing* *105*

Definitive Indicators   107

THIRTEEN   *How a Brokerage Firm Reports Technical Data* *109*

FOURTEEN   *How to Find Winning Stocks* *112*

Check the Historical Pattern   116
Relative Strength Approach   118

FIFTEEN   *How to Use Technical Analysis to Time Selling* *121*

Successful Selling   122
Be Willing to Take a Small, Quick Loss   125
Summary   126

SIXTEEN   *How to Make Money in Bear Markets by Selling Short*   *128*

Technique of Short Selling   129
Using Technical Indicators   129
Finding Stocks to Sell Short   130
Rules for Successful Short Selling   132

SEVENTEEN   *How to Use Stop Orders Successfully* *135*

Other Critical Points   137
Stop-Limit Orders   139

EIGHTEEN   *Technical Analysis and Options: Useful but Not Essential* *141*

Buying Options   142
Special Options Charts   143
Computerized Premium Returns   146

NINETEEN   *Technical Analysis with Commodities Futures Trading*   *147*

Importance of a Speculator   148
Technical Indicators Aid Pyramiding   151
Point & Figure Chart of Commodities   152

TWENTY *Technical Rules and Lore* *155*

Rules for Technical Analysis   155
Stock Market Lore   157

Glossary of Investment, Stock Market and Technical Terms   161
References   176
Index   181

Acknowledgments

Thanks for help in writing this guide go to many people:

GEORGE H. BROOKS, G. H. Brooks Associates, Inc., of Bridgeport, Connecticut, for his professional counsel and guidance in editing the manuscript

KENNETH WARD, the late veteran technician who introduced me to charts and technical analysis

RICHARD BLACKMAN, President of Richard Blackman & Co., Inc., for his sound advice, especially on selling

JACK MAURER, President of *Indicator Digest*, who provided many charts and interpretations

WILLIAM L. JILER, President of Commodity Research Bureau, Inc., for one of the best books on charts

JOSEPH E. GRANVILLE, Author of two excellent books on technical analysis

HARVEY A. KROW, Author but now retired

JOHN MAGEE, Author of the standard professional text

JOHN WINTHROP WRIGHT, President of Wright Investors' Service, Bridgeport, Connecticut, for his concepts of fundamental analysis

I also received special assistance from:

S. ALAN BECKER, Securities Research Company

A. W. Cohen, Chartcraft, Inc.

James Dines, James Dines & Co., Inc.

Norman B. Fosback, The Institute for Econometric Research

Edson Gould, Investment adviser

Leroy H. Gross, Dean Witter Reynolds Securities, Inc.

Kenneth W. Lutz, President of Trendline

Arthur A. Merrill, Merrill's Technical Trends

Richard Russell, Dow Theory Letters

John Schulz, Brean Murray & Co.

Robert Stovall, Dean Witter Reynolds Securities, Inc.

Stan Weinstein, The Professional Tape Reader

Don Worden, Worden & Worden

Disclaimer

Every attempt has been made to verify the accuracy of the figures and statements. If there are discrepancies, it is probably because of different interpretations by different technicians or the use of statistics of different dates or conditions. This is a guide, not a text. It is written to show amateur investors how to use and profit by various types of technical analysis.

*The Investor's Guide
to Technical Analysis*

ONE

How Technical Analysis Can Boost Stock Market Profits

In the stock market there are two broad approaches to investment success: fundamental analysis and technical analysis. Both have strong champions. Both can make money for investors who do their homework, get the facts, watch developments carefully and act quickly, decisively and with common sense.

When combined, they can provide all the tools needed to make money in the stock and commodities markets:

- Fundamental analysis to determine the quality and value of stocks, bonds and commodities contracts
- Technical analysis to aid in the selection of specific securities, to improve timing of buying and selling and to boost profits and reduce losses

My own experience is that, properly interpreted, technical analysis can raise total investment returns (income plus capital gains and less losses) from 10% to over 15% a year. These results were with quality stocks in the erratic markets of 1976–1977. Amateurs who are willing to spend the time to *manage* their portfolios can do as well and, in a strong market, should do even better.

There are scores of excellent books on fundamental analysis but only a handful on technical analysis, and with few exceptions, these are either so outdated or so complex that they are not of much use to most investors.

This book is designed to provide a guide for the amateur investor; it describes and explains technical analysis in terms which any intelligent individual can relate to his or her investment strategy and can use to preserve capital and to make money with savings.

A PRACTICAL TOOL

There was a time when technical analysis was regarded as one step removed from reading tea leaves for portents of the future. There still exists a good deal of mysticism, much of it encouraged by specialists who sell charts and technical services. But as you will learn in the chapters ahead, technical analysis is a logical, easy-to-understand approach to the stock and commodities markets.

Some technicians have developed complex calculations and esoteric theories, but the basic concepts are simple. Technical analysis is a study of supply and demand as shown by the action of the market itself. This, in turn, is the best indicator of the future course of the market, stock groups and specific issues.

Today technical analysis is an accepted part of effective money management. Almost every successful institutional investment organization has at least one technician on its staff; there are scores of technically based advisory services, and thousands of people consult charts and other indicators before making their investment/trading decisions. Everyone who owns securities should have at least a working knowledge of technical analysis. That's the objective of this guide.

Don't get the idea that technical analysis is a surefire system to guarantee investment success. It is not. But according to practitioners and my own experience, it works 80% of the time.

No one technical indicator can provide all the answers. Charts are the most graphic and effective tool. But the final decision requires a consensus of indicators: moving averages, highs and lows, Advance/Decline line, short interest and other readily available stock market statistics.

Primarily, the technician relies on trends. The technician knows that a trend in motion is assumed intact until it ends; if a stock is moving up, it will continue to rise until there's a clear reversal, and vice versa for a down trending stock.

Trends can be spotted on charts, and because they are based on market action, charts do not lie. The patterns show the changes in the equilibrium of supply and demand and form the basis for trendlines. To the technician, it makes no difference whether there is a logical reason for the market action. Of interest is the *what*, not the *why*.

An upmove, especially with higher volume, means that large buyers are optimistic. This may be the time to buy. If the trend is down and the volume rises, it's probably a sell signal.

HISTORY OF TECHNICAL ANALYSIS

Broadly speaking, technical analysis is based on a doctrine called the *Dow Theory*. This was developed from editorials written by Charles H. Dow in *The Wall Street Journal* at the turn of the century. As will be explained later, Dow and his disciples saw the stock market as being made up of two types of waves: (1) primary, multiyear ebbs and flows and (2) secondary, short-duration movements. These can be recorded and interpreted on charts.

The action of the stock market is measured by Dow Averages composed of major stocks in three groups: Industrials, Transportation and Utilities. Very few technicians take significant positions against the trend of the Dow Averages.

Specific technical indicators, such as charts of individual stocks and moving averages, started to be used in the early 1920s by a handful of analysts who felt that valuable information could be obtained from the action of the market itself. They recognized the importance of trends and gradually developed indicators of past and current market and stock action to aid in predicting the future. According to one of these pioneers, Kenneth Ward, the original use of technical analysis was to protect the investor against loss. Convinced that the primary goal of all investing was to preserve capital, he developed technical data to determine the probabilities of stock market action and, eventually, stock action.

Since those years the field has been broadened, and with the aid of fast-calculating computers, it now involves scores of different indicators.

TECHNICAL VERSUS FUNDAMENTAL ANALYSIS

Since most people are uncertain as to the role of technical analysis, let's make a broad comparison by assuming that the fundamentalist is a conservative who invests for the long term and the technician is a trader who buys and sells for short-term profits. Actually, of course, the value of technical analysis lies between these extremes.

Fundamentalists study the cause, not the "should." They make their decisions on quality, value and, depending on their specific investment goals, the yield or growth potential of the security. They are concerned with the basics: the corporation's financial strength, record of growth in sales and earnings, profitability, investment acceptance and so on. They also take into account the general business and market conditions. Finally, they interpret these data inductively to determine the current value of the stock and then to project its future price. Fundamentalists are patient and seldom expect meaningful profits in less than one year.

In the long run, the fundamentalist who selects quality stocks when they are undervalued and sells them when they become fully priced will make substantial profits. But as John Maynard Keynes often noted, "In the long run, we'll all be dead."

Compared with long-term investors, technicians seek to keep their money working as profitably as possible at all times. When trading, they want to score profits quickly, and if the stock or market does not perform as anticipated, they are willing to take a small, fast loss.

Technically oriented investors start by checking the market action of the stock. If it's favorable, they examine the fundamentals to be sure the company is sound and profitable. At all times their focus is on the market: generally, on the performance of all listed stocks; specifically, on the price/volume movement of the stock they are considering buying. They make their decision on technical, not fundamental, data.

Technicians believe that (1) the stock market is rooted 15% in economics and 85% in psychology; (2) the record of past and present performance of a stock, not necessarily of the corporation, is the key factor; and (3) Wall Street, dominated by institutional investors, operates on the wolf pack theory of following the leaders. When major money managers start to buy, regardless of the reason, the price of the stock will go up. When they start to sell, it will do down. All such moves are shown by technical indicators.

In more detailed terms, here are several ways the technician thinks and acts.

1. *Technicians believe that behind the fundamentals are important factors.* At any given time, some investors have gains in the stock, and usually, some have losses. Those with gains want to safeguard them and, if possible, build them higher. They will hold the stock.

Those with losses will adopt different tactics: Some will cut their losses short by selling out early when the stock price begins to decline; others will sell when a minor rally has moved the stock up to their cost price; and still others will hold on doggedly until there's a turnaround.

Each of these decision points can be spotted on charts: current configurations to show the action of the past week or so; intermediate- and long-term patterns to find the previous important price levels at which selling is likely; and interim and long-term high points from which the stock started to move down in the past.

In this method of analysis, a vital factor is volume. Volume is favorable on the upside when the number of shares traded is greater than before, and on the downside when the number of shares traded dwindles. Volume is unfavorable when volume dips as prices rise or increases when there's a decline. None of these indicators are concerned with the fundamentals of the corporation.

2. *Technicians act on the* **what** *not the* **why.** They recognize that formations and patterns signify changes in real value as the result of investor expectations, hopes, fears, industry developments and so on. They are not as impressed with the fundamental value of any security as they are with the current and prospective values reflected by market action.

3. *Technicians are not committed to a buy-and-hold policy.* As long as the trend is up, they will hold a stock. This may be for months or even years. But if there's a reversal, they will sell within hours of purchase. They recognize that, to achieve the greatest gains, they must never let sentiment or emotion override facts (as shown by technical indicators) and should always get out of a situation which, on available evidence, is no longer profitable.

4. *Technicians do not separate income from capital gains.* They look for total returns, that is, the realized price less the price paid plus dividends received.

This is a sharp contrast to most long-term investors who buy a high-dividend-paying stock and hold it for years, through up-and-down fluctuations. To the technician, such strategy is foolish. A stock may continue to pay liberally but lose 50% of its value. If a stock is to be judged solely on its income, a nondividend payer, such as Crown Cork & Seal, would have no value at all.

5. *Technicians act more quickly to make commitments and to take profits or losses.* They are not concerned with maintaining a position in any market, any industry or any stock. As a result, they are willing to take smaller gains in an up market and accept quick losses in a down market. Traders/technicians want to keep their money working at maximum efficiency.

Technicians know that there is no real value to any stock and that price reflects supply and demand, which are governed by hundreds of factors, rational and irrational. No one can grasp and weigh them all, but to a surprising degree, the market does so automatically.

6. *Technicians recognize that the more experience one has with the technical indicators, the more alert one becomes to the pitfalls and failures of investing.* To

be rewarding, technical analysis requires attention and discipline. With quality stocks held for the long term, time can make up for timing mistakes. With technical approaches, the errors become clear quickly.

7. **Technicians insist that the market always repeats.** What has happened before will probably be repeated again; therefore, current movements can be used for future projections.

With all markets and almost all stocks, there are cycles and trends. Those of the past will occur again and again. Technical analysis, especially charts, provides the best and most convenient method of comparison.

8. **Technicians believe that breakouts from previous trends are important signals.** They indicate a shift in that all-important supply and demand. When confirmed, breakouts are almost always accurate signals to buy or sell.

9. **Technicians recognize that the securities of a strong company are often weak and those of a weak company may be strong.** Technical analysis can quickly show when such situations occur. These indicators always delineate between the company and the stock.

10. **Technicians use charts to confirm fundamentals.** When both agree, the odds are favorable for a profitable movement if the trend of the overall stock market is also favorable.

NEGATIVES OF TECHNICAL ANALYSIS

Let me repeat: Technical analysis is not, by itself, the road to riches. It is a tool which should be used with fundamental analysis and, most important, with common sense. Despite assertions of some technicians, technical analysis is still an art. Successful use requires talent, judgment, intuition and experience. Add a little luck, and it can be the difference between modest and good profits.

As you will see for yourself, some technical theories are more plausible than profitable. They may work under some conditions but can cause substantial losses under others. In many cases, there is little margin for safety. The signals are either right or wrong. If the signal, or your interpretation of it, is wrong, you lose money.

Some other disadvantages of technical analysis include the following:

1. All data used in technical analysis is past. Therefore, these indices cannot take into account unexpected events such as natural disasters and economic crises. Charts can, however, show activity by insiders well before privileged information becomes public knowledge.

2. With actively traded stocks, the prices may be the result of a battle of wits. For the most part, trading profits are realized at the expense of others who are trying to achieve gains on their own terms. In such cases, the technician must be cleverer and luckier than his or her rivals.

3. False signals can occur. A chart may show a sudden, deep decline which, by strict interpretation, is a signal to sell. But this may be the result of one large trade at a lower-than-market price. The value of the stock may bounce back quickly. If the technician failed to wait for confirmation, commissions would have to be paid for the sale and, probably, for repurchase.

4. The technical action of the stock may reflect buying and selling based on inaccurate information, such as incorrect forecast of earnings or industry prospects.

5. Technical indicators are mechanical and therefore subject to errors, breakdowns and misinterpretation. According to Benjamin Graham, dean of stock market philosophers, "With technical analysis, rewards can be realized more quickly, but, in the long run, may be more disappointing than those based on fundamental analysis. There is no dependable way of making money easily and quickly in Wall Street or anywhere else."[1]

That's a good reason to combine the two basic approaches: Put your money in quality stocks, and buy and sell them on the basis of technical analysis.

ABOUT THIS GUIDE

Technical analysis is such a broad field that, to fit the limited pages of this book, some areas have been summarized and others omitted. The examples were selected to provide the amateur investor with enough knowledge to utilize readily available technical information and to make better use of special advisory services.

If you become sufficiently interested to want more detailed explanations of technical theories and techniques, read the books listed in the references, work with a technically skilled broker or ask for regular reports from a firm's technical research department.

Always look upon technical analysis as another important tool in successful investment practice. By combining fundamental and technical

---

[1]Benjamin Graham et al., *Security Analysis* (New York: McGraw-Hill, 1962).

analysis, every intelligent investor should be able to attain average annual total returns—income plus appreciation—of 10% and, with experience and a favorable stock market, 15% or more on invested capital.

If that sounds unrealistic, remember that over 40 years, 1926–1965, the total returns of *all* common stocks listed with the New York Stock Exchange (NYSE), compounded annually, averaged 9.3% a year. If you stick to quality stocks and use technical analysis wisely, you can reach that 15% target and, by prompt reinvestment of all income and gains, double your money every five years.

Now let's find out how this goal can be achieved.

TWO

Stock Market Theories and Their Use

DOW THEORY

Behind every management technique is a rationale—an approach often started as a theory but usually proven by facts over the years. In technical analysis of the stock market, that basic concept is the Dow Theory.

The Dow Theory is named after Charles H. Dow, one of the founders of Dow, Jones & Company, Inc., the financial reporting and publishing organization. It is the most widely used of all theories concerned with securities. Mr. Dow never published a formal treatise, so most of the interpretations were developed by his successors, notably W. P. Hamilton, Robert Rhea and G. W. Bishop, Jr.

To Dow, the stock market was a barometer of business. His theory calls the turns of the market and forecasts the business cycle or longer periods of prosperity or depression. Under his concept, there are two major movements of the stock market: the *primary* movement, which lasts from one year to 28–33 months or longer; and the *secondary* movement, which usually lasts from three weeks to three months and, during this period, retraces one-third to two-thirds of the previous market action—the advance in a bull market, the decline in a bear market.

These movements are like giant waves within which are ebbs and flows that, in turn, may contain smaller waves and ripples. Like the sea, the stock market is always moving and, ultimately, always reversing. The objective of the Dow theorists is the correct determination of these movements. Day-to-day fluctuations, in either direction, are of minor interest except as they make up the longer-term waves.

Basically, the Dow Theory states that the trend of the stock market is confirmed only when both the Dow Jones Industrial Average (DJIA) and the Dow Jones Transportation Average (DJTA) surpass previous peaks or fall below previous lows. Once that trend is established, the stock market will continue in the same direction until canceled by reverse actions by both of these indicators. Confirmation need not occur in the same day. The moves of the averages may vary in strength but not in direction.

As explained by Robert Rhea, "Successive rallies penetrating preceding high points with ensuing declines terminating above preceding low points, offer a bullish indication."[1] Vice versa for a bearish indication.

A rally or decline, under the Dow interpretation, is one or more daily movements resulting in the reversal of direction exceeding 3% of either average.

When movements of both averages hold within a range of about 4% for several weeks, a *line* is said to have been formed. Whether this reflects accumulation or distribution depends on the succeeding action. If both averages break out above this line, it was accumulation and therefore higher prices are ahead. If the averages break out below the line, the reverse conclusions are deduced. Action by one average, unconfirmed by the other, is not conclusive.

The Dow Theory does not apply to individual stock selections or analysis. It is a guideline only to the action of the overall market. Specific issues will rise or fall with the averages most of the time, but any particular security may be affected by special conditions.

Often Difficult to Interpret

The Dow Theory leaves no room for sentiment. Its internal movements are often difficult to interpret, but its long-term movements are relatively concise and have been accurate over the years.

A primary bear market does not end until there have been three distinct steps:

---

[1]Quoted in George W. Bishop, *Charles H. Dow and the Dow Theory* (Englewood Cliffs, N. J.: Appleton Century Crofts, Inc., 1960), p. 228

1. "The abandonment of hopes upon which stocks were purchased at inflated prices"[2]
2. Selling due to lower corporate sales and earnings
3. Distress selling of securities regardless of value

A primary bull market requires three similar but opposite steps:

1. A broad upmovement, interrrupted by secondary reactions averaging longer than two years, with successive rallies rising above the peak of the previous intermediate rises and ensuing declines halting above the bottom of the previous intermediate declines
2. An advance in stock prices, with increasing volume, as the result of greater demand resulting from improved business conditions
3. Rampant speculation when the prices of stocks soar, based more on hopes than on facts

Note: Keep these steps in mind when you review the history of the stock market in recent years. Such understanding will help you have patience to wait for similar patterns in the future.

These broad swings may take years. It's a slow, often painful (for the investor) process. In a bull market, there's an upmove, then a drop back of one- to two-thirds, then another upmove, etc. It's the opposite with bear markets.

Secondary Movements

The most difficult to interpret (and accept) actions are the secondary ebbs and flows. These occur when the market bounces around with no visible base or support area. In bear markets they can be especially tricky because they may be mistaken for a reversal of the primary trend. Explains Rhea, "Traders and market experts become very bullish" and, frustrated by the slow movement, lose faith and "become bearish just about the time the real upturn comes." Yet, he adds, "These secondary reactions are as necessary to the stock market as safety valves are to steam boilers. They dampen the speculative ardor of amateur traders . . . correct a move which has gone too far in one direction."[3]

Review the Pattern

The best way to grasp the Dow Theory is to review past charts to see how these predicated patterns worked out: in a bear market, two or more

---

[2]Perry P. Greiner, "The Dow Theory: An Anthology," *Encyclopedia of Stock Market Techniques* (Larchmont, N. Y.: Investors' Intelligence, Inc., 1965).

[3]Quoted in Bishop (digested).

downward legs in primary swings and at least one secondary reaction, for example, late 1973 and mid-1974 with the reaction in between.

On the upside, an example would be the long upsurge in early 1975, the relatively stable period and then the sharp rise in early 1976. This time the plateau was longer but, despite some sharp dips, showed no signs of a bear market decline at the start of 1977.

The most recent primary bull market was signaled on January 27, 1975, when the Dow Jones Industrial Average closed at 692.66, thereby surpassing the previous rally peak of 674.75 of November 5, 1974. Confirmation came when the Dow Jones Transportation Average closed at 156.70, just above its November 7 peak of 156.61. In the entire 78-year history of the Dow Averages, this type of reversal pattern has never failed to signal a new primary bull market. In March 1977 the DJIA was in the 960 area and the DJTA was up to around 227.

Dow Averages

The statistical data used to record the movements of the stock market and for plotting charts are the three Dow Averages. These are calculated by adding the prices of selected NYSE-listed stocks and dividing by a divisor. This last figure is changed whenever one of the stocks is split, when there has been a stock dividend of at least 10% or when a new stock is substituted for one on the list.

Dow Jones Industrial Average (DJIA): 30 major industrial corporations, such as AT&T, Exxon Corporation, General Electric, General Motors, Sears Roebuck and U.S. Steel. Recently, the divisor was 1.504.

Dow Jones Transportation Average (DJTA): 20 transportation companies, such as American Airlines, Chessie System, McLean Trucking Company, Mississippi River Co. and Santa Fe Industries. Divisor: 2.567.

Dow Jones Utilities Average (DJUA): 15 electrical and gas companies, including American Electric Power, Consolidated Edison, Houston Light & Power, Public Service Electric and Gas and Southern California Edison. Divisor: 3.912.

Doubting the Dow

Critics fault the Dow Theory because they feel the averages have the following drawbacks:

The averages are outdated. The stock market is vastly different than when the theory was initiated and expanded. There are thousands more publicly owned corporations, millions more investors and the *daily* volume on the NYSE is half as much as the *annual* trading at the turn of the century.

The averages are no longer relevant. The current 30 companies, expanded from the original 12, are not representative of today's technologically oriented and service-concentrated business corporations. General Electric is the only survivor of the original average; IBM, the dominant investment, is no longer included; and the substitution of Minnesota Mining & Manufacturing for Anaconda Co. (now part of Atlantic Richfield) was a belated recognition of modern trends.

The Transportation Average is outmoded because of the substitution of airlines and trucking companies for railroads. When first selected, rails mirrored business activity, but no more.

The averages use closing prices. The averages, as published daily, reflect only the closing prices of the stocks. Yet the intraday advances or declines may be greater. As a result, trends are not always accurate unless the technician goes to the trouble of getting the special hourly reports.

The averages may be too late. By the time the Dow Averages have signaled a bull or bear market, one-third to one-half of the move has already taken place.

The averages are no help to intermediate-term investors (seeking profits in a year or so). To properly utilize the Dow Theory, it is necessary to view the market over a two- or three-year period. This is difficult for experienced investors and almost impossible for newcomers.

To repeat: The Dow Theory is the basis of pure technical analysis of the stock market. It reflects the *is*, not *what ought to be*. The chart of the DJIA is the number 1 tool for investors. It shows trends and, when properly interpreted, can provide meaningful projections of the stock market. For the long term, it is essential; for the intermediate term, it is valuable; for the short term, it is useful.

As is shown throughout this book, to make worthwhile profits in the stock market, the technician buys only when the trend of the market is moving up (or, if you are aggressive, appears to be ready to do so); sells, or gets ready to sell, when the trend is down; and sells short when a decline is confirmed.

These are tough rules to follow. Conservative investors will hold on to quality securities knowing that, eventually, the market will turn and value will be recognized. More aggressive investors will wince at the cost of commissions to sell and reinvest the proceeds. They will forget that, for the

Chart 2.1 STOCK MARKET PRICE AND VOLUME

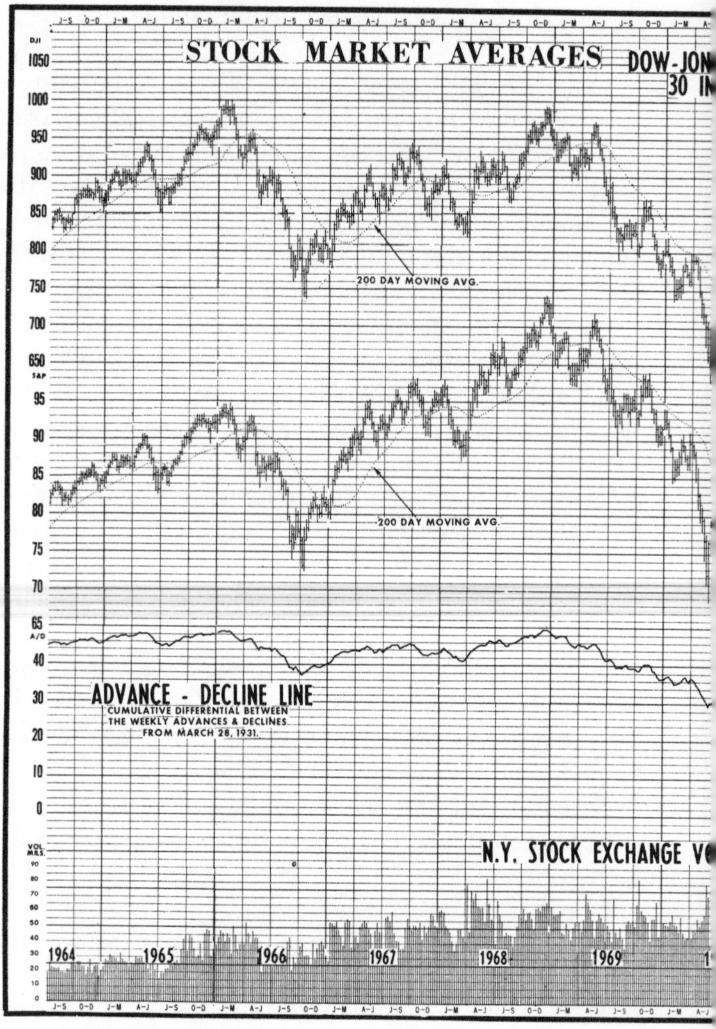

STOCK MARKET AVERAGES DOW-JON 30 IN

200 DAY MOVING AVG.

200 DAY MOVING AVG.

ADVANCE - DECLINE LINE
CUMULATIVE DIFFERENTIAL BETWEEN
THE WEEKLY ADVANCES & DECLINES
FROM MARCH 28, 1931.

N.Y. STOCK EXCHANGE V

1964 1965 1966 1967 1968 1969

SOURCE: Trendline, Inc.

average stock, a two-point drop will be as much as the cost of a round trip transaction. Traders who try to buck the market will end up broke.

Whether or not you accept the Dow Theory and use it in determining your investment strategy, it is still a strong force in Wall Street. When enough people believe in a particular theory, their own actions will make it come true—partially, anyway.

One thing is certain: The stock market itself is the single most important

STANDARD & POOR'S
COMPOSITE INDEX OF 500 STOCKS

technical indicator. Over the years it has stayed about six months ahead of the economy. This knowledge can mean the difference between modest and really rewarding profits—or losses.

Using Stock Market Averages

In charting, the two most widely used averages are the Dow Jones Industrials and Standard & Poor's Composite Index of 500 Stocks. Both have disadvantages but are useful as general market guides as standards of comparison for actions of stock groups, specific equities and technical indicators such as moving averages and Advance/Decline lines, as shown by Chart 2.1. They report the trends.

To make meaningful comparisons, it's important to understand the composition of the Dow Jones Industrial Average (DJIA) and Standard & Poor's Composite Index of 500 Stocks, the most widely used indices. Both indices include only stocks listed on the New York Stock Exchange. Similar averages are available for stocks listed on the American Stock Exchange (AMEX) and for those traded Over-the-Counter (OTC).

The DJIA is calculated by dividing the total prices of the 30 giant corporations by an often changing divisor. Quotations are reported every half hour during the trading day.

Over the years the DJIA has moved up, with wide and frequent fluctuations. In 1929 it reached 399, it fell to a low of 41 in 1932, then it rose erratically: to 153 in 1940, to 235 in 1950, to 685 in 1960, to 995 in 1966, to a record 1052 in 1973 and then down and up again to close at 1005 in 1976.

The DJIA is numerically limited and weighted so it cannot accurately reflect the actual percentage change in the prices of all stocks traded on the NYSE. The weight of each stock is proportional to its market value; for example, a 10% decline in a high-priced issue such as DuPont, from 150 to 135, has 5 times as much weight as a similar 10% drop in a lower-priced stock such as Woolworth, from 30 to 27. Thus, it would take a 50% rise in Woolworth, from 30 to 45, to offset a 10% dip in DuPont.

Furthermore, each split or stock dividend, which changes the divisor, lessens the weight of the stock by reducing its per share price. This tends to lower the long-term growth rate of the DJIA below that of all NYSE stocks. Over the years this creates a not-too-accurate comparison with past averages: i.e., a 1000 high in 1976 was really lower than the same figure in 1972.

Standard & Poor's 500 Stock Index reports the market actions of the stocks of major corporations: 425 Industrials, 20 Railroads and 55 Utilities. This also is a weighted average. Each stock's price is multiplied by the number of outstanding shares of common stock. The total is divided by the average market value during the base period, 1941–1943, and finally, multiplied by 10. (See Chart 2.2.)

Because it uses the total shares outstanding as the multiplying factor, stock dividends and splits have no effect. The major handicap of S&P's 500 is that some 50 large companies account for about one-half of the total market value.

Chart 2.2   FOR COMPARISON

To compare the DJIA with S&P's 500, multiply S&P's figures by 10. If the disparity with the DJIA is positive, the outlook is bearish. If it is increasingly negative, the forecast is bullish.

Use this handy measuring device when the DJIA walks alone to a new high or low. Usually, this will be the result of sharp price action by two or three Dow stocks. This is the time to check the overall market with S&P's 500.

Keep in mind that both of these averages do *not* reflect the movement of the average stock. They are selective, but they do show trends, which basically is the key to the successful use of technical analysis.

The New York Stock Exchange Common Stock Index, a composite of all NYSE common stocks, is also weighted. Unweighted averages are published by Value Line and *Indicator Digest*.

ELLIOTT WAVE THEORY: FOR LONG-TERM FORECASTING

One of the most accurate long-term technical indicators is the Elliott Wave Theory. This can be used with both securities and commodities markets

Chart 2.3   ELLIOTT WAVE THEORY

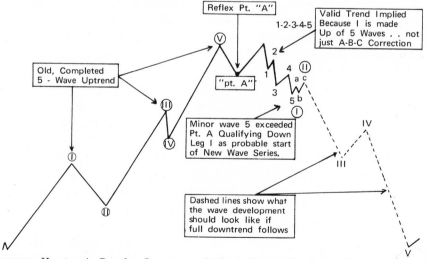

SOURCE: Houston A. Cox, Jr., *Concepts on Profits in Commodity Futures Trading* (New York: Reynolds Securities, Inc., 1972).

and with specific investment/speculative situations. It is complex, requires frequent updating and careful interpretation and, generally, is considered more of a philosophy than a theory. Since the end of World War II, it has been one of the most successful technical tools.

Developed by R. N. Elliott, the theory is similar to the Dow Theory in that it relies on broad movements or waves. The premise is that bull and bear markets are governed by natural law expressed in cyclical waves which repeat themselves in the same rhythmic patterns: five movements with three separate waves in the direction of the major trend and two corrective swings against that trend. (See Chart 2.3.) The pattern applies to both up and down markets.

For effective timing, compare this formation with the chart of intermediate-term (12–36 months) and long-term (up to 30 years) movements.

In interpreting this theory, it's important to have clearly defined, confirmed waves, to catch reversal points and to respect the signals under all circumstances.

The key is the counting of the waves and the identification of the reflex point which occurs after a previous five-wave major trend has been completed. There must be a full five-point count: 1, 2, 3, 4, 5. Three or four points are not enough. They may mean that the old trend is resting and will continue soon.

Note that the five upmoves (I through V) contain three strong rises and two diminishing reactions. In real life, there are scores of minor fluctuations within the broad trends. The confirmation of the reversal, at V, is when the dip goes below point A and thus signals a sure downleg and the probable start of a new wave series.

When the short, minor wave 5 drops below point A, this is confirmation of a further decline that can be projected by dashed lines.

In using the Elliott Theory in trading commodities, experts pay special attention to the three-wave, bunched formation (a,b,c) which precedes a long, strong reversal.

One weakness of the Elliott Theory is the lack of built-in measurement devices, but a good rule of thumb is that the second major move, up or down, in the direction of the major trend must be longer than the first and third moves, as it is on the upside and can be projected on the decline.

This is the kind of theory that is useful when you are familiar with charts and invest over a period of time long enough to establish broad patterns. Says one Elliott Wave enthusiast, "Waves don't end where they look like they're going. You must constantly check and recheck but once you see a pattern developing, it will be accurate 75% of the time for intermediate term and 90% for the long-term."[4]

Most amateurs prefer to use the DJIA or S&P's 500 as the base for their technical analysis. They are readily available, relatively easy to understand and quite convenient for comparisons, on charts and by figures. Both provide the background for major stock market movements.

[4]Personal interview by C. Colburn Hardy with staff of *Indicator Digest*, July 1974.

How to Plot Charts

Of all the technical indicators, charts are the most valuable and the easiest to use. They are graphic, factual and adaptable for review and projections. They are road maps to help you to figure out the best way to get from where you are to where you want to go (or not go). They are the working tools of technical analysis. They report what has happened in the marketplace as the result of supply and demand. Charts do not lie, but their interpretation varies with the skill and experience of the investor/trader.

The greatest value of charts is their ability to depict trends. Since a trend in motion remains intact until there is a distinct change, the configuration on the chart can be projected to indicate probable future action of the market, of groups or of specific stocks. Charts are essential to successful technical analysis but as James Dines, a leading technician, warns, "Charts are like fire or electricity. They are brilliant tools if intelligently controlled and handled but dangerous to a novice."[1] Well, that's true, but not if you use your common sense and do not try to rely solely on chart action.

The easiest way to learn about charts is to subscribe to a technical service which provides printed charts. (See References.) These are available for all NYSE- and AMEX-listed companies and for many OTC issues in three

[1]Personal interview by C. Colburn Hardy with James Dines, November 1974.

forms: daily, weekly and monthly covering time periods from six months to 12 years.

Technicians use all three: the first to spot current trends for buying and selling, the second to provide background and the third as a frame of reference for historical trends and market action.

The basic concept of charting is that patterns tend to be repeated; that is, what happened before will occur again. This reflects the fact that each stock has a personality of its own. Certain stocks are bought by certain types of people. AT&T, for example, is a favorite of trust funds and older individuals. Its stock makes few false, erratic or confusing moves.

Gulf & Western Industries, on the other hand, is more popular with speculators. Its action is characterized by sharp, wide moves, up and down. The chart shows these patterns clearly.

Charts also indicate important areas of support and resistance. The support level forms the base for an upside breakout. Resistance occurs at previously significant points, i.e., the price from which a stock started a decline.

When a stock drops from 20 to 15 and then starts to rise again, that 20 price is important. This is the area where the recovery usually will falter. Investors who bought at this price will be ready to sell to break even. Supply will become greater than demand, and the stock will probably go down until this supply is exhausted and the buyers become dominant again.

As technical tools, charts are easy to interpret for broad, long-term profits, but they may be difficult for amateurs seeking short-term gains.

A good way to start to learn how to use charts is to plot your own. First, get chart paper. You need plain squares for Point and Figure (P&F) charts, and logarithmic or standard paper for Bar charts.

POINT AND FIGURE CHARTS

P&F charts are one-dimensional. They show only price changes in relation to previous price changes. There are no indications of time or volume. In interpretation, the key factor is the change in price direction. P&F charts are favored by many professionals but, generally, are not as useful for amateurs.

To make a P&F chart, post the stock price in a square, one above another, depending on the direction of the price movement. Usually the unit of change is one point, but it can be less or more: ½ point for short-term trading, 2 or 3 points for longer projections. As long as the price continues in the same direction, the same column is used. When the price shifts its trend, move to the next column.

In the financial press, find the price action of the average/group/stock which you want to chart. For routine charts, use only the closing price. The opening quotation is seldom significant in estimating the future.

Stock	Sales	High	Low	Last	Net Change
GenMot	1469	66¾	65½	66	+¼

In this chart of GM (Chart 3.1), the stock fell from 68 to 67 to 66, then rose to 67, so the next entry was in column 2. As the price dropped, point by point, to 62, there was no change until the upmove to 63 when the next entry was in column 3, and so on.

John Schulz, who writes on technical analysis for *Forbes*, says that "For significant rendering of the underlying facts, nothing can beat a P&F chart."[2]

[2]John Schulz, "How to Forecast Stock and Market Action with Charts," *Forbes*, 1961.

Chart 3.1 POINT & FIGURE CHART: PLOTTING PRICE ACTION OF GENERAL MOTORS STOCK

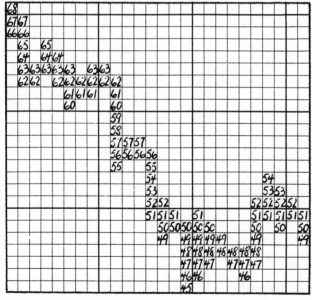

SOURCE: C. Colburn Hardy, *Your Investments*, 1977–1978 edition (New York: Thomas Y. Crowell, 1977).

In his view, the values of this type of chart are the following:

Price reversal. Successive price reversals link up to make trend reversals. Thus, two stocks, one of which reverses more frequently than the other, will produce different charts. This detailed information is difficult to obtain with Bar charts.

Predictive ability. Forecasting the carrying power of price changes is based on the sideways movement of the chart. "There is demonstrable cause and effect relationship between lateral action and subsequent vertical movement. . . . As a general proposition, the lateral extent of the price reversal in a trading range has a bearing on the carrying power that ensues when the trading range is finally resolved."[3]

Thus, to forecast the span of the probable vertical move, up or down, measure the preceding lateral movement. The longer that lateral trend remains in effect, the more stocks can move from sellers to buyers or vice versa. The strength and length of this upmove or downmove reflect the earlier buildup. Schulz believes this indicator is more accurate on the upside, since on the downside, there are always investors who will never sell their stock.

In the GM chart, the last buy signal came at the reversal around 48. This long lateral movement was followed by a relatively equal updrive to 54. The reversal, from 54 to 53, was a signal to sell—before the stock went down to 49.

Adds Schulz, "Watch for trends and reversals. Keep flexible. Use P&F charts to get the feel of a market or of a stock rather than as always-to-be-obeyed signals."[4]

Disadvantages of P&F Charts

These are drawbacks to this type of chart:

They do not portray intraday action. The information on the financial pages reports only the high, low and closing prices. Yet the stock might have moved up and down several times during the day.

Entries are usually in whole numbers. This misses some significant shifts in market evaluation.

There is no mention of volume. Many technicians feel that the number and trend of transactions are an important guide to investor interest. It's bullish if the price rise is accompanied by heavier trading or the decline occurs with dwindling volume.

[3]Ibid.
[4]Ibid.

The structure of the chart makes it difficult to draw trendlines and channels. These are both valuable for comparisons with past patterns.

There is no clear frame of reference to determine when to buy or sell, as with Bar charts.

Note: The best way to learn about P&F charts is to copy the chart of an active stock. With each entry, ask yourself, "Would I buy or sell or hold at this point?" After a while, you can transfer this knowledge to new situations.

BAR CHARTS

For best results with Bar charts, use special logarithmic paper. This permits charts to be plotted on a semilogarithmic scale. A two-cycle scale has the value printed on the margin, from 1 to 100. The logo scale means that the

Chart 3.2 DAILY BAR CHART

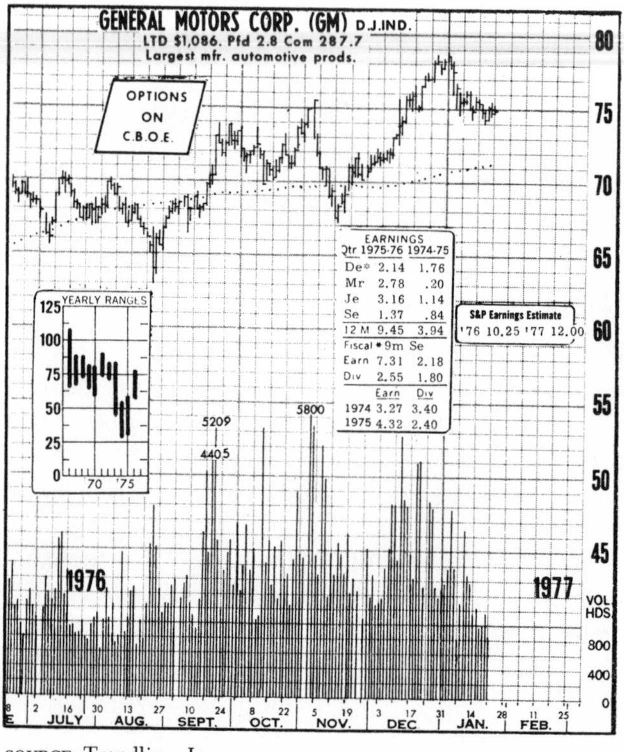

SOURCE: Trendline, Inc.

Chart 3.3 12-YEAR CHART

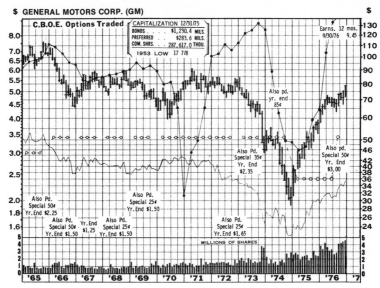

SOURCE: Securities Research Company, Inc.

measured distance between any two numbers depends on the ratio between the two numbers, not the arithmetic difference. Thus, the spread between 2 and 4 is the same as between 4 and 8, or 100%.

The chart paper does the computing. Changes due to a stock split, stock dividend, etc., are noted by multiplying or dividing the scale printed on the margin, not by adding or subtracting.

To build a Bar chart, enter a dot representing the highest price at which the stock traded on that day, week or month; then enter another dot for the low. Connect the dots and add a horizontal nub to mark the closing price.

Study Charts 3.2 and 3.3 and refer to them as you learn more about technical analysis. Keep in mind that GM is a tremendous force in the American economy. It is the world's largest privately managed, publicly owned corporation. It is well-managed and, historically, has been extremely profitable with a Profit Rate (return on stockholder's equity) averaging over 16% a year. That's 50% greater than the profitability of the 30 stocks which make up the DJIA (of which GM is a component). Dividends have been ample, from a low of $2.40 to $8.34 per share.

Yet there have been wide fluctuations in the value of this quality stock, from an adjusted high of 113¾ in 1965 to a low of 28⅞ in 1974.

What better example can there be of why you should not buy a stock and store it away? By fundamental analysis, GM has always scored high. Only rarely has it been so overvalued that it should have been sold. But the investor who bought on basic values, even at a median price, would have lost a lot of money over the years. If the investor had paid attention to technical analysis, he or she would have sold and bought GM at least 10 and probably a dozen times in the 12 years reviewed on the long-term chart!

How to Read a Chart

Chart 4.1 is typical of the data available from printed services (see References). It covers weekly activity for an intermediate term of four years. Most analysts also check two other charts: *short-term charts*, plotted daily for up to two years; and *long-term charts*, with monthly data for 12 years. For amateurs, the first and last are sufficient.

Each firm has its own special format/indicators, but the configurations and information are similar. Houston Oil & Minerals Corp. (HOI) is an integrated petroleum company whose stock is traded on the AMEX. The chart shows a long, relatively flat period from 1973 through 1975. The upmove starts in late 1975 and, from then on, with a few downskips, drives to a record high of 56, with adjustments for 5-for-4 and 2-for-1 splits. This is the kind of stock where technical analysis, and especially a chart, is very valuable. It shows trends, flashes signals and is easy to follow.

Charts prepared by services provide both an overview of the market action of the stock and statistical data on the company's financial strength and operating results. Here are explanations of the numbers:

    1. *Industry group.* One of the 60 categories used to aid in evaluation of comparable corporations.

    2. *Corporate description.* Major products, services, interests.

    3. *Price action.* For the week, the horizontal line indicates the closing

Chart 4.1 EXAMPLE OF A MASTER CHART

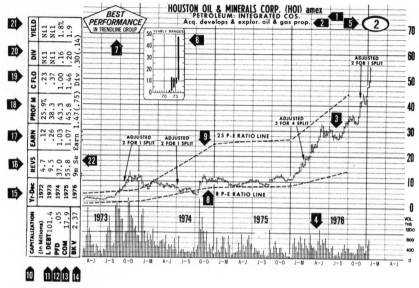

SOURCE: Trendline, Inc.

price of the stock; the vertical line depicts the range of price movements. In early December 1976 there was a big, one-day jump from about 36 to 40. Such sharp activity is usually a sign of better things to come.

4. *Volume* (at the bottom). The vertical line shows the number of shares traded during the week. Here the scale (on the right side) is 1,000 shares, so in the last week, just under 800,000 shares changed hands.

5. *Performance ranking*. This is another *Trendline* feature. It ranks 972 stocks as to their comparative price action for the calendar year. In this case, HOI was number 2.

6. *Yearly range chart*. The vertical lines on this insert represent the yearly range of the price movement, adjusted for splits and major stock dividends. This is a quick guide to the market action of the stock under review.

7. *Best performance in Trendline group*. This is a designation given only to the stock which currently shows the largest percentage price appreciation in each of the 60 industry groups.

8. 9. *Price Earnings (P/E) ratio lines*. These are also *Trendline* specials. They indicate the approximate price at which the stock would be selling at its historic multiples: (8) a low P/E of 8; (9) a high P/E of 25. These

lines are valuable to determine whether a stock is under- or overvalued and to set target prices for sale. In this case, HOI is above its highest historical range and, most analysts believe, at a level where it should either be sold or watched carefully.

10. 11. 12. 13. *Capitalization* (lower left box). This shows the total long-term liabilities, in millions of dollars ($101.4), and outstanding shares, in millions: 0.05 preferred and 17.9 common.

The long-term debt represents loans that mature more than one year ahead as stated in the last financial statement.

14. *Book value*. The net worth (assets minus liabilities) per share of common stock: $2.37. Only a few stocks sell far above book value.

15. *Years*. December shows the last month of the company's fiscal year.

16. *Revenues*. Reported income, usually sales, for the stated year.

17. *Earnings*. In dollars per common share. Here there's been a sharp advance, from 12¢ in 1972 to $1.07 in 1975 and, for nine months of 1976, $1.47.

18. *Profit Margin (PM)*. This is obtained by dividing net earnings per share (before taxes) by sales per share. This is a general measure of corporate profitability. With HOI, the PM nearly doubled in four years, from 25.9% to 45.8%.

19. *Cash Flow*. Net income, in dollars per share, plus noncash charges such as depreciation, depletion and amortization, up sevenfold from $0.23 million to $1.46 million.

20. *Dividends*. The dollars, per common share, paid out in the fiscal year. *Nil* indicates that no dividend was declared in 1972 and 1973. A stock dividend would be shown in percentages.

21. *Yield*. The dividend as a percentage of the average market price of the stock for the fiscal year.

22. *Latest earnings, dividends and year-ago comparisons*. 9m Se Earn 1.47 (.75) Div. 20 (.14) means that, for the nine-month period ending the last day of September, the earnings per share were $1.47 compared with 75¢ for the same period of the previous year. Dividends were 30¢ per share this year versus 14¢ in 1975.

Note: There are special definitions for finance companies, insurance firms, investment companies, railroads, utilities and savings and loan associations.

FIVE

The Importance of Trendlines

Trendlines are the single most important tool in chart analysis. Properly used, they can improve timing to maximize profits and minimize losses. They are easy to plot, not too difficult to interpret and are almost always reliable when confirmed.

An uptrendline (see Chart 5.1) is formed by using a rule and sharp pencil to draw a straight line connecting the last two or three *low* prices. This establishes the base and becomes the support level to provide a frame of reference for buying an up stock and selling a down one.

Downtrendlines (see Chart 5.1) are the opposite. They are drawn by connecting the last two or three *tops*. Since they show a down pattern, they indicate stocks which should be bought only for short sales.

Once a trendline is formed, the stock will probably (but not certainly) move along that line. Even when there's a breakaway, there's a tendency for the stock to return to its established pattern.

For profits in normal and bull markets, look for uptrendlines. They always point to possible gains. They predict the trend and they provide a base for buying and, when projected, target areas for selling. The earlier in

Chart 5.1   TYPES OF TRENDLINES

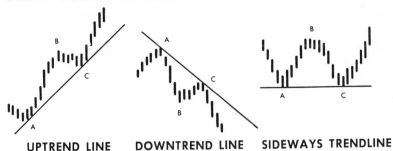

UPTREND LINE   DOWNTREND LINE   SIDEWAYS TRENDLINE

SOURCE: William L. Jiler, *How Charts Can Help You in the Stock Market* (New York: Trendline, Inc., 1972).

the formation of an uptrendline and the closer to the actual line you buy, the greater will be your profit.

For profits in bear markets, look for downtrendlines. They indicate possible gains by selling short.

The *only* stocks to consider buying are those which are moving up and have a potential for substantial gains: 25% to 50% for long-term investments and 15% to 25% for short-term trading. The trendlines show these movements and possibilities.

The key to the successful use of these technical indicators, says Richard Blackman, is "Buy only *up* stocks in *up* groups in an *up* market."[1]

The trendline is a traffic signal. As long as it is up, the light is green; when there's a break, the light is amber so be cautious; when it reverses, it's a red signal to get ready to sell.

The longer the trendline, the more reliable it is. Thus, a trendline is more valuable on a weekly than on a daily chart; on a monthly report than on a weekly one; on a yearly chart than on a monthly one. Once that trendline holds, preferably for a month but occasionally for less, it can be expected to be maintained and can predict future market action. But even a strong trendline needs help from the overall market.

Curiously, nearly all minor, most intermediate and many primary trends follow straight lines. They are a visual recitation of the Dow Theory with its ebbs, flows and major waves. The ripples are the movements above the trendline in what may become a channel.

With a declining stock, the trendline is not likely to be quite as straight, but can be used just as effectively to time short sales.

[1]Richard Blackman, *Follow the Leaders* (New York: Simon and Schuster, 1977).

WHAT TO WATCH FOR IN TRENDLINES

Not all trendlines have equal validity. The more volatile the stock, the easier to spot and follow the trendline. But it's also more risky, because reversals can come quickly and move rapidly. The signals are easiest to catch with a high flyer like Tandy Corp.

Length. The longer the trendline remains intact, the greater the technical significance. But all good things must come to an end. On the Tandy chart (see Chart 5.2), the steep, relatively long advance came in November–December 1975 with an upmove from the low 20s to the high 40s. When the reversal came, it was sharp and retraced about half the gain.

Spacing. The more widely spaced the bottoms, the more likely the

Chart 5.2   USING TRENDLINES

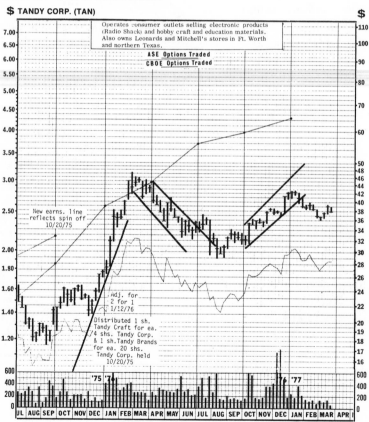

$ TANDY CORP. (TAN)

Operates consumer outlets selling electronic products (Radio Shack) and hobby craft and education materials. Also owns Leonards and Mitchell's stores in Ft. Worth and northern Texas.

ASE Options Traded
CBOE Options Traded

New earns. line reflects spin off 10/20/75

Adj. for 2 for 1 1/12/76

Distributed 1 sh. Tandy Craft for ea. 4 shs. Tandy Corp. & 1 sh. Tandy Brands for ea. 20 shs. Tandy Corp. held 10/20/75

SOURCE: Securities Research Company, Inc.

trend will be carried out. When lows come close together, change can come quickly. With Tandy, the narrow distance between the August and September 1975 lows predicted a short, aborted rise—this took place and then was followed by a new upswing.

Angle. The steeper the angle of the trendline, the less meaningful it is. A steep line can mean fast gains, but it can be broken easily by a sudden sidemove and the subsequent trend will probably continue at a slower pace. With Tandy, the almost vertical updrive in December 1974–January 1975 did not last long, and the angle of the next downturn was less and that of the late-year upmove was far less steep and lasted longer.

These sharp moves take place with temporarily popular, actively traded stocks. Buyers want to get aboard at any price. Usually, the top comes suddenly, and as the Dow Chemical chart shows, the pattern does not touch the original trendline for some time.

The lower the angle, the more valid the trend. See both charts of GM. The moves are quite long and, with the exception of the oil-crisis panic, stay within a relatively narrow range.

Time. The building of the upmove is closely related to the action of the overall market. In a bullish period, the updrive may be completed in six to eight weeks (as with Tandy). In a flat or erratic market, the move can take months.

Watch the time span of small reversals. If they take place during the upmove, they are not likely to be significant. But if a short shift occurs at the start of a new formation, it may be a clue as to the probable trend development.

Number of Testings. Watch how frequently the trendline is tested. Two-point trendlines are common. When there's a third, as in Chart 5.3, an upside breakthrough is likely. This works on the downside too.

Chart 5.3 TESTING TRENDLINES

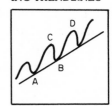

SOURCE: The Professional Tape Reader.

Note: If the stock holds in that second stage for some time, the ultimate breakout in a strong market may be substantial. Many times you have to be *very* patient. If the trend stays up, it will probably be worth waiting for.

Penetration. It is imperative that the penetration, on the downside or upside, be real. In erratic markets, there can be interim fluctuations which will spill over and then pull back. This can be rough on the uninitiated who buy a trading stock and then watch it drop below the trendline.

The trend of the overall market is very important. If it's really down and your stock holds fairly well, you probably should hold on and hope. But if the stock dips with the market, a decisive sell penetration should have these characteristics:

- Be more than 3% (1½ points for a stock at 50) or, in a strong bull market, 5% (2½ points).
- Last more than one day, though not necessarily consecutively.
- Be accompanied by heavier volume on the upside but not so important on the downside. However, if the break is decisive—2 or more points—volume is not important.
- Hold at or close to the new peak. If the price drops back and closes nearer the bottom of the channel on the same day, the volume should ebb too.

LONG-TERM TRENDS

The trendline is especially valuable when a stock has a long rise, as with Dow Chemical. As the price keeps going up and up, you become worried about when to sell. As long as the uptrendline is not penetrated, hold on. But when the downbreak comes, as it did with Dow in 1973, sell fast at 30.

If you still like the company, buy back in after the inevitable pullback, at around 24 (adjusted for splits). (See Chart 6.14.)

Note the resistance which developed when the stock rose to 46 in mid-1975. After some consolidation, there was another short rise to 57¼. But the new trendline was penetrated at 50 in early 1976. Then, Dow was no longer an up stock.

Note, too, that the more stable the stock, the less likely are sharp reversals. Top quality stocks, like Dow and GM, seldom retrace 50% of their previous advances. With a volatile issue, like Tandy, the moves are steep and fast and the 50% rule applies (see page 52).

Interpret charts on the basis of the character of the shareowners: with GM, conservative, long-term investors; with Dow, a mixture of conservative and aggressive investors; with Tandy, aggressive, short-term traders.

VARIATIONS OF TRENDLINES

Trendlines can also be drawn on P&F charts. Here's a special variation used by Chartcraft, Inc. (see Chart 5.4). Here the price changes are recorded by standard P&F practice: X's when the move is up; O's when it's down. Each is in a separate column. The digits (9,7,8, etc.) report the daily high or low when at a whole number.

Chart 5.4 POINT AND FIGURE CHARTS: BULLISH AND BEARISH

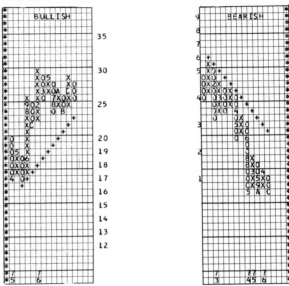

SOURCE: Chartcraft, Inc.

The trendlines are marked by small X's. These are drawn by intersecting successive squares, up or down, not by connecting two price points.

The Bullish Support Line is drawn from a low point immediately after the first upturn. It is tentative until there are two columns of price changes above this trendline. The Bearish Resistance Line is the opposite: drawn downward from a high point on the chart immediately after the first downturn.

In both cases, the Support Line will disappear when it is touched by a reversal of the price change.

Advises Chartcraft, "If you are long, hold as long as the Bullish Support Line is not penetrated. If you sold short, hold until there's a break through the Bearish Resistance Line.

"The best stocks to buy are those which: (1) have given a buy signal by penetrating a previous top; (2) have a valid Bullish Support Line and (3) do not have a valid Bearish Resistance Line.

"The best stocks to sell short are those which: (1) have given a sell signal by penetration of a previous bottom; (2) have a valid Bearish Resistance Line and (3) have no valid Bullish Support Lines."[2]

[2]The Chartcraft Point & Figure Chart Book, Larchmont, N.Y., Chartcraft, Inc., February 1977, p. 4.

———————————————————————

SIX

Chart Patterns: Plain and Fancy

Chart patterns are like music. There are scores of variations on a theme. Some, with titillating titles such as Prussian Helmet, Megaphone Top or Tombstone Bottom, provide excellent publicity for advisory services; others are the products of someone's fascination with numbers; and still others involve explanations that might persuade you that they hold the alchemist's secret of producing gold. But not many of the originators/promoters of these special configurations are millionaires.

The basic chart patterns, however, have considerable validity and can be used profitably. The trick is to let them help, but not dominate, your decision making. In this chapter, some of the most widely used and easily recognizable chart patterns are presented. Their values are what you want to make of them. Some technicians swear by them, but most successful practitioners regard them as supplements to other information and as confirmation of signals provided by trendlines. Even if you do not always rely on them to aid your investment timing, you can enjoy the excitement of spotting them on charts.

Note: These are *typical* chart patterns. Study them to learn how they report what's happening and how they may signal the future. Always use your common sense, consider the consequences if your interpretation is wrong and look for confirmation by other technical indicators.

THE RELIABLE V FORMATION

The V formation is just what the name indicates: a long, sharp decline; a fast, short reversal; and a 45° upmove, usually above or close to the previous high. It is one of the most reliable, most exciting and most profitable chart formations. They are always easy to spot.

Typically, V's develop with volatile, popular stocks where investor interest swings rapidly from hope to fear and back again. An inverted V is similar, except the rise comes first and the decline last.

There are also extended V's where the bottom (or top) moves more slowly over a broader area, sometimes before and sometimes after the pivot point.

With most V's, everything happens quickly. The downtrend is steep, the reversal area is as short as one day and the climb is as precipitous as the decline, though usually with more backing and filling. Occasionally, in dull markets, the changes come more slowly and gradually. But the pattern is always clear: a shift in investor sentiment.

Polaroid Corp. (PRD) is a good example of the type of stock whose market action creates V patterns (see Chart 6.1). When it's popular, its price soars; when it's unpopular, the decline is fast and steep. These moves are so predictable that they can be used to make money by buying long on the updrive, and selling short with the fall.

In late 1969 PRD hit a new high above 140, then plummeted almost straight down to the mid-50s. Within a week, the stock was on its way up again and, in less than a year, recovered over 60 points. Then came another short, squatty V and a comeback to a record high of 149½. For more than a year, there was a period of erratic consolidation before a break down to 130 and then the V formation again as the stock fell almost straight down. The pivot came at just over 14. After a few fits and starts, the right side developed as the stock pushed up to 43½, experienced another consolidation and—well, if past is prologue, the V will extend in the next several years.

Note how narrow the fluctuations were. During the 1970-1971 upsweep, the trendline was never broken until after the reversal. In the same way, the downtrend in 1973–1974 was almost perpendicular. In both situations, the reversals came in a very short time, four months in 1971 and less in 1974.

Chart 6.1   V FORMATION

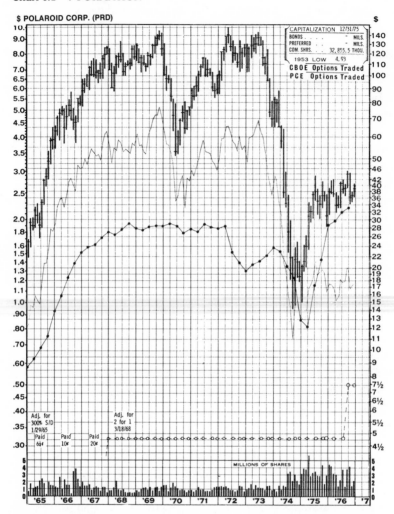

SOURCE: Securities Research Company, Inc.

Since stocks tend to repeat patterns, keep a close watch for charts with clear V patterns. Be cautious at bottoms (and tops if you sell short), and wait for confirmation. There will still be plenty of time for profits. And if you are a trader, you can move in and out on fluctuations because you are always sure of the primary trend.

Obviously, V formations are ideal for short selling. Forget about exact timing or maximum gains. Cover your position in the middle of the decline or, better, set mental buy stops. Throughout, watch for reversals and preserve your profits.

TOPS AND BOTTOMS

Picking tops and bottoms is interesting but not important. What you want to get is the middle move: to buy after the uptrend has begun and to sell before the top has been reached. If a stock goes up 35%, you can afford to forget the first and last 5% moves. A 25% gain is ample. If you can achieve this four times a year, you will double your capital every 12 months.

Tops and bottoms are formed at the end or beginning of new trends. They always involve a reversal and usually will be followed by a continuing trend.

You do not have to wait for a specific pattern to form. If you use trend-lines, you may be able to sell before the exact top or buy after the exact bottom.

There are, however, guidelines to help you locate these key points. Technician John Magee acts cautiously and sets stop levels when a stock has moved "three days away" from the day marking what you suspect is the high or low. If a stock moves slowly down, makes a low of 24 and then moves up, Magee waits for three days when the stock holds above 25⅛. This may be confirmation. With tops, he uses a reverse standard.

For extra protection, the three-day range must always be below the entire range of the day making the new interim high, or with a top, below the day's quotations.

Once the stock stays at or above 25⅛, there's a new base point from which to make projections.

Making Decisions

With both bottoms and tops, the time for decision is when the stock makes a substantial (15% or more) move in the primary direction. Then it will usually retrace 40% of the distance from the previous base, and a new rise (or fall) will start. If this move is less than 40%, wait for a week or so to see if a new base point is established. Fluctuations do not always occur quickly, and in a strong upmove, it takes time for the stock to build a support level.

As a general rule, volume is more important with tops than with bottoms. In most cases, tops build quickly, but many fall apart just as fast. Typically, stocks will move within a narrow range at a top and then suddenly start to decline. As the drop continues, volume will increase. Once the decline is confirmed, the Big Boys will sell as much as fast as they can. The rout can be on. For individual investors, the best action is to sell before the peak.

With bottoms, the building is gradual and the volume erratic. Once the new trend is confirmed, trading may expand, but this takes time. People are slow to be convinced, especially after they have suffered losses on the downswing. Do not be in a hurry. Wait until you are sure of the bottom and the upturn.

Double Tops and Bottoms

These are always significant patterns. As a general rule, they signal the end of one trend and the start of another. They illustrate why it is so important to wait for a bottom or top to be confirmed.

A Double Bottom is formed when a stock falls to a certain level, usually with high value; then advances with diminishing activity; falls again to the same or, more likely, a lower price; and finally, turns up, probably for a major rise, possibly for an intermediate one. The pattern looks like the letter W (see Chart 6.2).

A Double Top is similar on the upside. Its pattern resembles the letter M.

Usually, these formations take three steps, as shown in the sketch of the DJIA in 1970: a downmove from 811 to 744, and a short, fairly steep rise to 791, a point lower than that from which the original decline started. The first confirmation comes with another, longer decline to 631. At the reversal, the stock moves up quite steadily and sharply past the previous checkpoints. An aggressive trader might start buying at around 700; a more conservative investor would probably wait a bit longer to be sure the trend is likely to continue.

Chart 6.2   W FORMATION

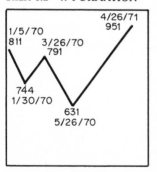

SOURCE: *New York Magazine.*

Both of these multiple formations are tricky. Very few formations that start out looking like Double Bottoms or Double Tops end up as true patterns.

This is logical. A stock normally meets resistance at a previous high and support at a previous low. In both cases, the normal pattern calls for a pullback, then a hesitation and then a continuation of the previous move.

Watch the volume. If the reversals are accompanied by heavy trading, the formations may be valid. But if the demand dwindles on the first swing, be cautious. The next step may be another, unexpected reversal through what had been considered a support level on the downside, a resistance area on the upside.

John Magee points out that Double Tops which come to about the same level in a short span of time with only minor reactions are likely to be part of a consolidation pattern and therefore not important moves. He is especially wary of patterns which form slowly (peaks a month or more apart) with little vitality. The danger signal is flashed when the declines go below the previous lows.

On the other hand, most technicians view Double Bottoms as a bullish sign and a prelude to a significant rise. Use All Double Tops and Bottoms as a frame of reference. Always wait for confirmation, and to be extra safe, draw in trend lines.

Patterns can also be formed by other technical indicators, such as the Advance/Decline line shown in Chart 6.3.

These are just as valuable signals/reference points as those to be found on charts of market averages or individual stocks.

Once in a great while, there will be Triple Tops and Triple Bottoms. If you watch your charts carefully, you will sell at the peaks and buy back at the bottoms. But it's not easy.

Checkpoints:

With all multiple Bottoms and Tops, ask these questions:

- Did the price shift 5% or more from the first peak or low?
- Was there unusual volume on the first move?
- What does the historical pattern of the chart show?
- At high points? at low points? Resistance levels? Support areas?
- Is the trend with or against that of the overall market?

A favorable answer to all these will minimize your risk. But it will not guarantee a profit.

Chart 6.3   ADVANCE/DECLINE LINE

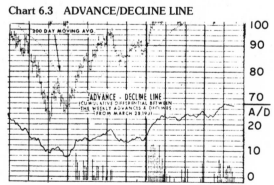

SOURCE: Trendline, Inc.

HEAD & SHOULDERS: MORE FUN
THAN PROFIT

This is the best-known.and most widely used reversal pattern. It's easy to spot and follow, and generally, its signals are reliable.

The Head & Shoulders (H&S) chart pattern (Chart 6.4) resembles the real thing: three successive rallies consisting of a Left Shoulder, a Head and a Right Shoulder. In between are dips. The end of a major uptrend comes when the chart of the right figure fails to reach the height of the center and heads downward.

What happens is this: The development of the Left Shoulder represents an upturn of some duration. The climax is reached with a strong rally. At this top, the people who bought during the uptrend start to sell. This creates an oversupply and the price of the stock drops—the first valley.

Near the base of this technical reaction, people who missed the first uptrend start to buy at relatively low prices. This creates a rally which pushes the stock up again to form the Head.

This second formation marks a new high and usually lasts for a longer period than either shoulder. Soon the sellers take charge again and push the price down so that most of the first move gain is erased. The bottom comes at or slightly below the previous valley. Normally, this volume is not as great as in the first Left Shoulder buildup/downswing.

The Right Shoulder is the third rally and peaks at a lower price than the Head and at about the same height as the first formation. Volume may

Chart 6.4 HEAD AND SHOULDERS CHART PATTERN

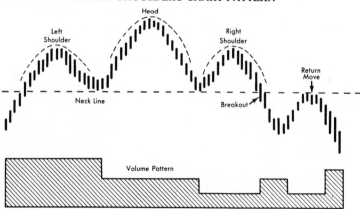

HEAD AND SHOULDERS TOP

SOURCE: William L. Jiler, *How Charts Can Help You in the Stock Market* (New York: Trendline, Inc., 1972).

Chart 6.5 HEAD & SHOULDERS

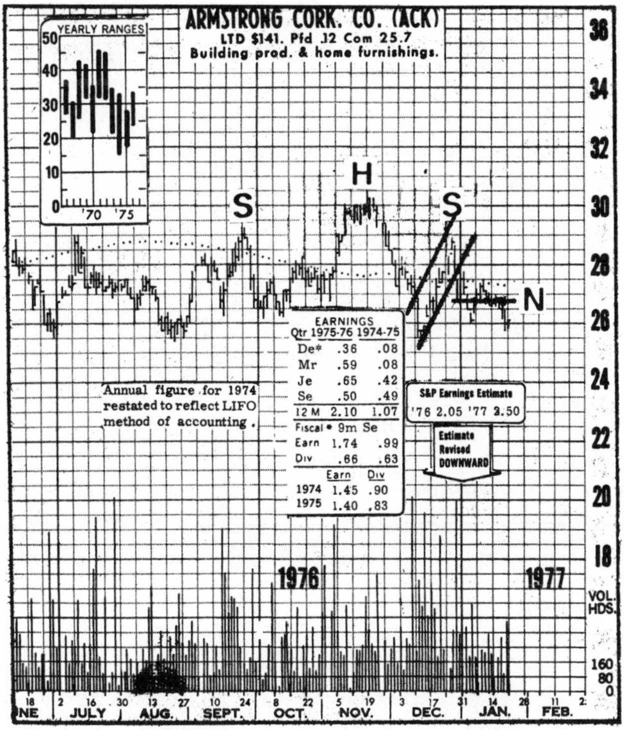
ARMSTRONG CORK. CO. (ACK)
LTD $141. Pfd .12 Com 25.7
Building prod. & home furnishings.
YEARLY RANGES
S
H
S
N
EARNINGS
Qtr 1975-76 1974-75
De* .36 .08
Mr .59 .08
Je .65 .42
Se .50 .49
12 M 2.10 1.07
Fiscal • 9m Se
Earn 1.74 .99
Div .66 .63
Earn Div
1974 1.45 .90
1975 1.40 .83
Annual figure for 1974 restated to reflect LIFO method of accounting.
S&P Earnings Estimate
'76 2.05 '77 2.50
Estimate Revised DOWNWARD
1976
1977
VOL. HDS.
JULY AUG. SEPT. OCT. NOV. DEC. JAN. FEB.

SOURCE: Trendline, Inc.

jump sporadically but, overall, will be less than those of the earlier patterns. The Right Shoulder development is the last chance for eager buyers. The drop comes when early buyers start to get out at a profit or, more likely, at a break-even point.

Note on Chart 6.5 of Armstrong Cork (ACK) how all moves involve frequent fluctuations yet follow well-defined trends.

Importance of the Neckline

The final sell signal comes when the price of the stock falls below the neckline. This is a horizontal line drawn at the bottom of the two previous lows. To the technician, no H&S is complete until this downbreak occurs.

This is the point when most sellers are anxious to bail out. There may be a technical rally which will stop at the neckline (not with ACK). But from then on, the decline starts. (See the N in Chart 6.5.)

In interpreting H&S charts, it is always important to watch the volume as compared with the normal number of transactions. Usually, but not always, it's highest on the original upmove, fairly stable during the middle formations, erratically high in building the Right Shoulder and strong again after the final downbreak. This depends, of course, on the overall market.

If the last downmove is followed by lower volume (as with ACK), there may be a pullback. This gives holders-on a last chance to get out with little or no loss.

Trendlines Better

To skeptics, the H&S pattern is an exercise in futility. Richard Blackman, for example, feels that the use of trendlines would dictate a sale at each peak and a buy after the valleys. *His argument:* Instead of waiting for the full H&S pattern to form, a shrewd trader could have scored three substantial profits and sustained no losses: "Like most fancy patterns, H&S is a better toy than profit-maker."[1]

If you do use H&S, do not wait for the final penetration of the neckline. Follow the formation and use trend lines to time your buying and selling.

FLAT PATTERNS

Some stocks, notably those of utilities, have such relatively stable operations that they tend to develop flat chart patterns because of price changes that are slow and small, rarely more than 5% a week. Such issues are poor candidates for trading. Technical analysis is useful primarily to improve investment timing.

American Natural Resources Co., a major utility, is a good example of a stock *not* to trade. This intermediate-term chart (Chart 6.6) shows why: a low of 30 in September 1975 and a high of 45 in December 1976 and, in between, small fluctuations.

With such stocks, charts catch only strong uptrends, such as the one which started in October 1976. If you were smart enough to buy at the absolute low of 36 and sell at the high of 45, you would have made a 25% profit. That's OK for an investment but not a large or quick enough gain to justify tying up trading capital for 15 months.

Stocks with flat charts are worth buying only for income or when the alternatives are risky and the group and the market are moving up. Even then, you'll probably have to set a low target: 15% gain with hopes for

---

[1]Personal interview by C. Colburn Hardy with Richard Blackman, manager of the Paramus, N.J., office of Herzfeld and Stern in October 1976.

Chart 6.6 FLAT PATTERN

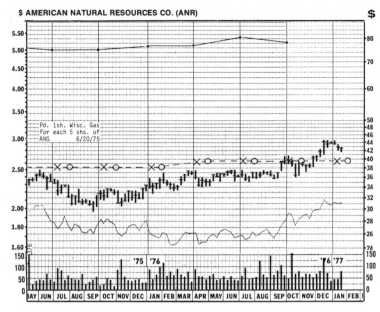

SOURCE: Securities Research Company, Inc.

more. In the meantime, however, you will probably get a dividend of 6% or more.

TRIANGLES ARE TRICKY

These easy-to-identify formations are one of the most popular technical patterns (see Chart 6.7). They are close cousins to pennants and flags. They can be tricky and are not always reliable. In most cases, they are more useful to professionals than to amateurs.

Chart 6.7 TRIANGLES

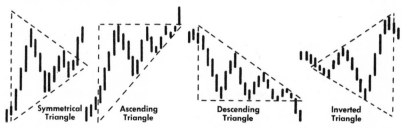

SOURCE: William L. Jiler, *How Charts Can Help You in the Stock Market* (New York: Trendline, Inc., 1972).

Triangles are another example of the complexities of true technical analysis. Fortunately for the less sophisticated, the same information signals can be obtained by simple-to-draw and simple-to-interpret trendlines.

Symmetrical Triangles These are composed of a series of price fluctuations, each smaller than its predecessor. The minor tops fail to attain the higher prices of the previous rallies, and the minor recessions stop above the level of the earlier bottoms. Thus, when trendlines are drawn, the boundaries tend to slant down or up to form a symmetrical, triangular pattern.

The value of such formations is their signal of a sharp break to come and their ability to measure the length of the ultimate (well, almost always so) move. Usually, this is as far as the width of the pattern development.

The trend of the triangle indicates that the market is making up its mind. There is no sure clue as to the direction of the breakout. As a general rule, there must be two minor tops to permit the drawing of the boundary line and four reversals to suggest the probable trend.

The traditional pattern calls for: (1) four minor advances, (2) a top, (3) four downswings to establish a bottom which is (4) higher than the original base and (5) a price movement away from the new bottom to create a meaningful triangle.

Says John Magee, "The best moves occur when prices break out decisively at a point somewhere between half and three-quarters of the horizontal distance from the base to the apex."[2]

Time is important because there's not likely to be sharp action if the prices continue to move sideways with ever narrower fluctuations. The stock runs out of steam. The best symmetrical triangles are tight ones.

Ascending Triangle Ideally, the top line of this pattern is horizontal and the bottom line slants up to form the triangle. The top line indicates the supply; the bottom, the demand. When demand overcomes supply, there will be a breakout from the ascending triangle. Volume should decrease as the pattern develops and increase at the breakout.

Descending Triangle This is the opposite of the above pattern and therefore usually forecasts a sharp decline. In the formation, the lower line indicates a support level. When there's a breakdown through that line, as shown by Chart 6.8 of Searle (G.D.), sell fast. A month later the stock was down another 15%.

[2]Personal conversation by C. Colburn Hardy with John Magee of John Magee, Springfield, Mass., in February 1977.

What happens is that, as sellers lower their ideas of value, the price slides toward the support level and eventually breaks through. Volume is important. The best situations show small volume during the formation and large trading with the breakout.

Inverted Triangle This is a funnel indicating investor nervousness and uncertainty. As the volume tends to increase, the price swings widen. Eventually, there's a breakout, usually on the downside.

With all stocks which develop triangles on their charts, there are likely to be repetitions over the years. It's the old story of all technical patterns.

Guidelines for Using Triangles

Here are William L. Jiler's guidelines on interpreting triangles:

- The odds favor a continuation of the trend that preceded the formation of the triangle.
- The likelihood of continuation of the inside-the-triangle pattern

Chart 6.8 DESCENDING TRIANGLE

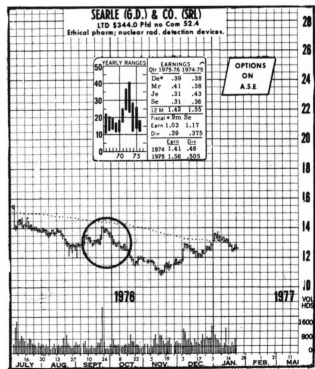

SOURCE: Trendline, Inc.

decreases according to which of the four formations develop, in this order: Ascending, Symmetrical, Descending and Inverted.

▪ Buy at the lowest possible level within the pattern and always after the triangle has become well-defined.

▪ Remember that all triangles are treacherous and subject to many false moves. Use them for reference rather than as sure signals.[3]

FLAGS AND PENNANTS

These are patterns that look like flags on a chart (see Chart 6.9). A pennant is a pointed flag. Before their formation, there is usually a flagstaff—a long, straight move. This is followed by a series of short price movements that extend or narrow with the changing trend. The signal comes with a breakout of the pattern, and almost always in the direction opposite that of the formation.

To be useful, the patterns must be tight and quick. In an up flag, the price fluctuations grow shorter to form a compact parallelogram which slopes back against the prevailing trend. The stock moves up and down with a narrow range with each new rally ending lower than the previous high and, usually, with diminishing volume. The next reaction carries the price slightly below the previous bottom, again with lower volume. Then comes a sharp rise, with greater trading, to a break through the top.

Flags form quickly. Each rally and setback may last only three or four days. The wider the pattern, the longer it will take to complete but usually, the maximum time for formation will be three weeks.

Pennants Flash Reliable Signals

A pennant is a pointed flag bounded by converging rather than parallel lines. The first movements are fairly broad but narrow in a few days. The

[3]William L. Jiler, *How Charts Can Help You in the Stock Market*, Trendline, Inc., New York, 120 (digested).

Chart 6.9 FLAGS AND PENNANTS

UP FLAG   DOWN FLAG   UP PENNANT   DOWN PENNANT

SOURCE: William L. Jiler, *How Charts Can Help You in the Stock Market* (New York: Trendline, Inc., 1972).

breakout comes when the daily price swings are small. Then, with high volume, the stock takes off, up or down, opposite to the early trend. The breakouts should occur two-thirds of the distance from the pole (the long, first line) to the projected point of the pennant. If the pattern spreads out too far, it is suspect and, usually, not to be acted upon.

With both flags and pennants, you can predict the ultimate gain or loss. To measure, go back to the start when the stock broke out of its consolidation or reversal pattern, the flagstaff. The distance from here to the breakout will approximate the length of the rise or fall. In most cases, the advance will be somewhat greater and the decline a little less than the yardstick.

Both flag and pennant formations are quite reliable, but to be sure of authenticity, John Magee suggests these checkpoints:

1. The consolidation should occur right after the straight line move.

2. Activity should diminish appreciably and constantly during construction and continue to decline until the breakout.

3. The price breakout, in the expected direction, should take place in not more than four weeks from the start of the flag formation. Be wary when it requires over three weeks.[4]

Flag at Half-Mast

When the "flag flies at half-mast"—consolidation at the halfway point—this can be a signal for a spectacular move ahead. There's likely to be a sustained drive with the second rise equal to the first. Usually, there's a reaction in the middle.

Do not become greedy when this pattern appears. After two surges, sell and let someone else try for profits.

Both flags and pennants are more effective with upmoving stocks than with declining ones. Such situations can be helpful in timing selling but not short selling.

GAPS CAN POINT TO PROFITS

Gaps represent a price range at which no shares changed hands. The stock opens one morning at a price much higher or lower (2 to 3 points) than the last price of the day before. When plotted on the chart, there's no price overlap, hence the term "gap."

Example: On October 14 Warner Communications (WCI) common

[4]John Magee, *Technical Analysis of Stock Trends* (Springfield, Mass.: John Magee, 1975), p. 177.

Chart 6.10   GAPS

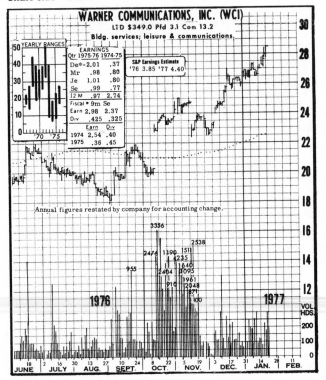

SOURCE: Trendline, Inc.

stock closed at 20½ (see Chart 6.10). The next morning it opened at 22½. In November the gap came on the downside.

Generally, the prior trend will continue: up with a rising stock as WCI was in October, and down with a failing stock as WCI was in November.

Gaps are most significant when they occur with an active stock. They usually precede a breakout and are almost always accurate in their forecasts. They indicate that the buying demand, or selling supply, is so strong that investors are willing to pay, or accept, an extra point or two than was quoted on the previous day.

Gaps are seldom meaningful with lightly traded stocks where a relatively large purchase or sale can cause a big swing.

Other types of gaps may occur when: (1) a stock becomes exhausted at the end of a rapid rise or fall (only rarely are such skips followed by major moves); (2) there's a breakaway, i.e., a sudden movement with heavy volume, after a chart pattern has been completed. This will widen the daily price range and cause an intraday gap.

Technicians disagree on how to interpret and utilize gaps. Old-timers insist that a gap must be filled—that the market will automatically rectify an error or enhance a major trend. Newcomers, accustomed to the fast action of computers and huge trading volumes, see the gap as an extension of already anticipated market action—overenthusiasm or overpessimism.

Whatever the explanation, the best use of gaps is for trading—picking up a few points by buying on the upbreak or by selling on the downgap. To most people, gaps add a bit of excitement to chart watching.

DON'T GET CAUGHT IN A TRAP

As in all business enterprises, there can be traps—unexpected situations which catch the unwary. In the stock market, these actions happen so quickly that they can be predicted only by daily charts (see Chart 6.11).

Traps represent a sharp, temporary change in investor sentiment. They may be part of normal pressure, but are more likely to be a ploy of major investors seeking to boost their profits or cut their losses.

A bull trap comes with a narrowly traded stock which suddenly breaks out to a new high from a fairly well-established support level. After a flurry of activity, the stock drops back sharply and usually falls right through the previous support area.

What may have happened is that a professional money manager who wants to get rid of his or her last 10,000 shares of Allied Soapdish enters small orders, perhaps 100–500 shares, with different brokers, at ever higher prices. This demand boosts the stock price to a new peak which attracts speculators.

At this point, the fund manager starts to sell his shares and gets out with a profit substantially greater than could have been achieved without the

Chart 6.11   TRAPS

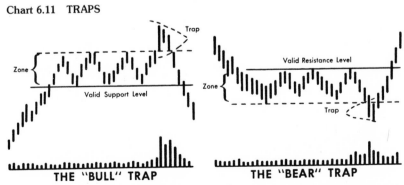

SOURCE: William L. Jiler, *How Charts Can Help You in the Stock Market* (New York: Trendline, Inc., 1972).

maneuvering. By the time the new buyers are ready to unload, there's no longer any demand. They have been caught in a bull trap.

The reverse, a bear trap, is less common but takes place in a similar manner when a stock drops suddenly to a new low with active trading and then bounces back through the previous resistance area.

In most cases, as the charts indicate, traps are followed by sharp swings of 10% to 25%. Over a longer term, they may cause such disillusionment that the stock will end with a major move of as much as 50%.

Advice: With a bull trap, traders should cash in and take their medicine or, if they are really daring, sell short. The best way to avoid being caught in any kind of trap is to wait for confirmation of the move and obey the signals of trend lines. When there's a downside break, get out fast. The next move can be much more costly.

50% RULE

When a stock moves up or down, there is likely to be a technical reaction which will lose or recover a good share of the move. This is the point at which traders act, taking quick profits in a rise and picking up bargains on a dip.

In longer swings, this support or resistance will be at a level midway of the previous move; i.e., a stock which jumps from 20 to 60 without a serious interruption and then backs off will lose about 50% of the 40-point gain and will find support at around 40, or 50% of the original rise.

This technical action is like a seesaw with the equilibrium at the 50% mark. When the stock moves above that 50% level, it is likely to keep going (like a teeterboard). Conversely, when it drops below that 50% level, it will continue to drop as far as it can. (See Chart 6.12.)

As a general rule, this 50% principle is most useful when measuring the

Chart 6.12   THE 50% RULE

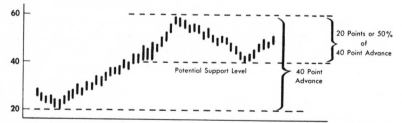

SOURCE: William L. Jiler, *How Charts Can Help You in the Stock Market* (New York: Trendline, Inc., 1972).

Chart 6.13   UNFAVORABLE PATTERNS

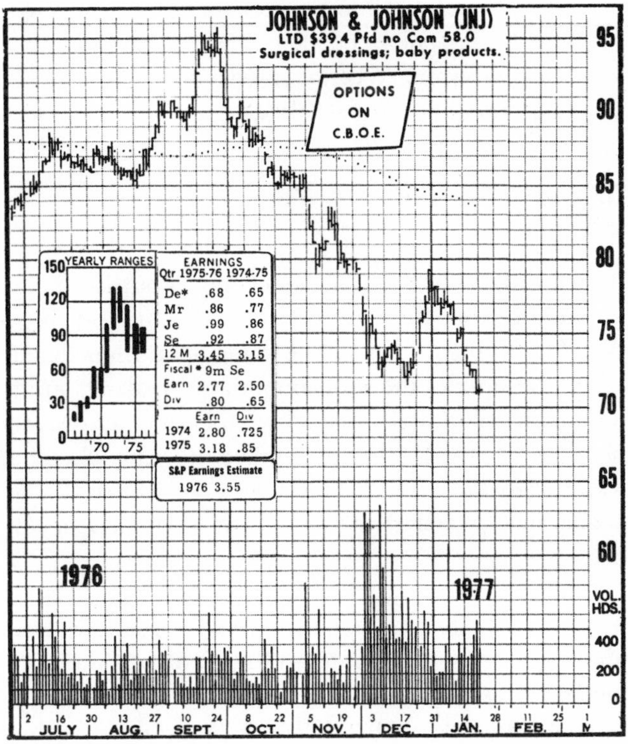

SOURCE: Trendline, Inc.

closing DJIA from its bear market low to its bull market high. Divide by 2, and you get the halfway level of the ensuing bear market.

The upward penetrations are slower than the downside ones. In bull markets, a climb may take as long as two years. In bear markets, the downside penetrations may occur in only three or four months.

Warning: Don't rely on this indicator in a bear market. You could be trapped.

UNFAVORABLE PATTERNS

Chart 6.13 shows a stock which, since the fall of 1976, should have been avoided, unless you were selling short. Investors have been unhappy about this once superglamour issue. Since September 1976 its price has gone almost straight down with heavy trading. There was an interim Double Bottom in December, a short rally and then another decline.

Despite the fact that the J&J is a top-quality company with a great record of profitable growth, it has been and, at this writing, still is a poor investment. It is unpopular and should be bought only by very optimistic, very long-term investors. When you see a down pattern like this, skip the chart page and look for uptrends elsewhere.

BREAKOUTS ARE ALWAYS IMPORTANT

A breakout occurs when the stock moves outside the trendline or channel. It indicates that there's been an important shift in supply and demand. When confirmed, it should be acted upon immediately.

On the upside, the most important breakouts are to interim and long-term highs. With both, the longer the time between the new and previous high, the greater the future upmove. Be wary when a new high is reached within a relatively short time, say, a year or so. There are still too many people who will start selling and thus dampen, if not destroy, the profit potential.

When the stock reaches a historic peak, this is almost always a *go* signal. At this point, all shareholders have a profit and will wait for a further rise. Major investors want more and more shares and are willing to pay ever higher prices. The stampede is on.

That's the rule, but as Chart 6.14 of Dow Chemical shows, there are exceptions: for example, in late 1973 when the stock ran up to 34, an all-time high. This record value was not sustained and, with an overall down market, fell sharply.

There were also new highs in late 1974. The first was so close to the previous peak that it had to be regarded as an interim high. The time span, less than nine months, was too short for a sustained drive. Sellers drove the price down.

The second interim high, a shade lower, came a few weeks later. Again, this was too short a time spread and was followed by a quick, steep dip.

All-Time High

A good example of the importance of the all-time high came, with Dow, in mid-1971 when the stock (at an adjusted price) broke above 15, the previous peak achieved more than three years before. With such a long time between highs, this upmove was an almost certain signal. The stock more than doubled in price in three years and kept rising (Chart 6.14).

Another Example

The chart of American Natural Resources Co. (Chart 6.6) is more graphic, showing an interim high at the end of 1970 after two years of meandering. The price held for a while, dropped with other utilities and, with tremendous volume, soared to its old peak in late 1972, a four-year time span. But the market fell off and the stock dropped back.

With quality stocks, new highs happen rarely. When there's heavy volume, there may be a pullback, but usually, a breakout is a favorable

Chart 6.14   BREAKOUTS

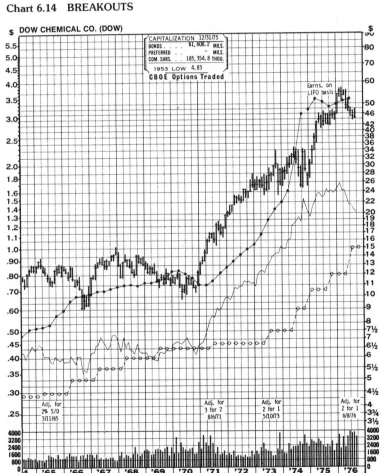

SOURCE: Securities Research Company, Inc.

sign. You can buy high and sell higher. The ultimate gain will be at least 20% and, often, 50%—as with Dow, which soared from around 12 to 57¼.

Note how important it is to keep the trend line up-to-date. With Dow, the old trend lines were broken at least once in every year from 1973 through 1976.

To Sell or Not to Sell

Technicians disagree on whether or not to sell at a breakout. They know that, while most breakouts are followed by higher prices, there are occasions when the penetration is short and is followed by a reaction and, frequently, by a downturn—especially in a down market.

With all types of breakouts, be prepared to follow the rules but stay flexible. In erratic or down markets, nail down your gains and keep close watch. In strong markets, you can let your profits run.

Here are some rules of thumb for decisions on breakouts:

- If you have a profit of 20% or more, sell part or all of your stock into the strength of the breakout. You are sure of finding a ready market. If the stock does continue to rise, you can buy back on the inevitable pullback *if* there is still a chance for a reasonable gain—at least 15%, and better, 25%.

- When a stock approaches an interim high, get ready to sell at the breakout. Hold only if the penetration is very strong and the market is bullish.

- If the market is surging up and the volume for the stock and its group is high, hold and set a mental stop at just above the breakout point, for example, at 18 for Dow when it moved over 15. Then review the situation when the new high is reached.

- If the market is flat or fluctuating, sell and take your profits.

- When you have taken a profit in one stock, check other equities in the same industry/group: i.e., if the breakout came with Holiday Inn, sell for a profit and switch to Howard Johnson if there is a chance for a reasonable profit in the new shares.

Fundamental versus Technical Analysis

These "rules" provide a good example of the difference between fundamental and technical analysis. To many fundamentalists, a new high may represent a target price at which, by historical standards, the stock has become fully priced. They would sell and look for other investments. Such a rigid policy would destroy the possibility of the big gains yet to come.

The technician might sell at, or close to, the breakout, but would not abandon the opportunity. He or she would buy back if the trendline continued up and market conditions were favorable. The technician knows that a trend will continue until there is a strong reason/pressure for a reversal.

Remember: The technician acts on what *is*; the fundamentalist acts on what *should be*.

Downside Breakouts

The rules for downside breakouts are not so flexible. When the stock slips below the trendline, get ready to sell. If the decline is confirmed, get out fast. There may be intermittent fluctuations, but once a stock loses favor with major investors, there's no way to know how far it will drop. AMF went from 67¼ to 9⅝; Xerox from 171⅞ to 46⅞; Avon from 140 to below 20—all in a couple of years.

USING HINDSIGHT

Interpreting charts long after the moves have taken place is easy. It's far more difficult to judge future action on the scene. To sharpen your forecasting, study old charts of stocks you plan to buy, and at each major move, ask yourself, "Would I buy, hold or sell?"

Soon you'll get the word and be able to score profits while your fundamentalist friends have lost their opportunity or are still hoping for their stocks to rise.

———————————————————

SEVEN

Forecasting Indicators for Strategy and Tactics

"Forecasting sows the seed; trading reaps the harvest." This is one Wall Street adage which makes sense and, generally, is true.

There are scores of technical forecasting devices/indicators. Some are valid, but many have been developed to sell investment advisory services. Most have enough validity to justify their use but are not sufficiently accurate to be relied upon alone. Their predictions may be 80% correct, but their mistakes can be costly. You can increase the odds for success by using several of these predicting tools and applying common sense when there are unusual distortions.

Technical forecasters can be helpful for both strategic and tactical investment decisions. They are more effective in projecting intermediate- and long-term trends than for trading. Predicting daily, weekly or even monthly market or stock action can be difficult, and too often you become so engrossed in the minor ups and downs that you lose sight of the primary trend.

Here are some of the most widely used forecasting indicators and several typical special formulas. They are supplementary tools which can be used to refine timing; they should not be used as substitutes for basic technical or fundamental analysis.

SEASONAL FORECASTERS

Within all cycles of markets and stock groups are seasonal movements which tend to follow fairly consistent patterns and, within broad limits, to forecast future activity.

January forecast. "As January goes, so goes the year." If the stock market, as measured by the DJIA or S&P's 500, rises in January, the December close will be at a higher level, and vice versa.

Skeptics feel that this indicator is more psychological than real, that a lot of changes can develop in the next 11 months and that the true value of this forecaster is the fact that when enough people believe something, it will become self-fulfilling.

Maybe so. But the record shows that in the past 21 years, the January Barometer has forecast the *course* of the stock market 80% of the time. (See Table 7.1.)

As with all technical tools, you have to add common sense. Later pressures can accelerate or change the market's interim direction, but the year-end results are what counts. In 1970 the January market action signaled a bad year. The market declined until late May, then recovered and, by December's close, was a fraction on the plus side. Those who heeded the January indicator profited; they did not buy stocks early in the year. If you have any faith in any technical indicators, pay attention to what happens in January, but temper your purchases, or lack of them, by watching other yardsticks during the year.

Five days' action. This is a subdivision of the January Forecast developed by Yale Hirsch, editor of *The Stock Trader's Almanac*. It predicates that the first five days of the new year are an early warning system that has been correct 88% of the time. Says Hirsch, "Since 1950, the first gains were matched during the year except in 1966 and 1973."[1]

In 1977 the first week's trading ended 2% below the 1976 close.

Summer rally. This rally, shown in Table 7.2, is one of the most dependable market movements. The odds are about 2:1 that the June opening prices will be lower than those of the end of August and 3:1 that they will be below the year-end close. On this basis, June is a good time to buy.

Post–Labor Day rally. This is based on the premise that, within a few weeks after this early fall holiday, investors make up their minds about the investment outlook. Their conclusions determine the course of the market for the rest of the year. Optimists buy; pessimists sell.

[1] Personal conversation by C. Colburn Hardy with staff member of The Hirsch Organization, Old Tappan, N.J., February 1977.

TABLE 7.1   January Indicator

	January change	Year change
Up years		
1952	+1.6%	+11.8%
1954	+5.1	+45.0
1955	+1.8	+26.4
1958	+4.3	+38.1
1959	+0.4	+8.5
1961	+6.3	+23.1
1963	+4.9	+18.9
1964	+2.7	+13.0
1965	+3.3	+9.1
1967	+7.8	+20.1
1971	+4.0	+10.8
1975	+12.3	+31.5
1976	+11.8	+18.0
Down years		
1953	−0.7	−6.6
1957	−4.2	−14.3
1960	−7.1	−3.0
1962	−3.8	−11.8
1969	−0.8	−11.4
1973	−1.7	−17.0
1974	−1.0	−29.7
Exceptions		
1956	−3.6	+2.6
1966	+0.5	−13.1
1968	−4.4	+7.7
1970	−7.6	+0.1

SOURCE: C. Colburn Hardy, *Your Investments*, 1977–1978 ed. (New York: Thomas Y. Crowell, 1977).

This is a case where the original theory appears to be valid but the longer-term results may not be so favorable. Over 15 years, there have been ten bull market advances and four bear market declines. By following this forecaster, you would have profited 71% of the time. But you would have done better if you had been patient: In three of those four declines, there were rises in the first few months of the next year.

Year-end rally. Seasonally, December is the strongest period of the year. Since 1897 the DJIA has risen in December 71% of the time and in 38 of the 79 years has reached an annual high.

BEST TIMES TO BUY

Heavy institutional activity has confused some traditional timing patterns, but here are some "best" times to buy or sell, as reflected in historical patterns.

Within any quarter. Buy just before the end of the reporting period for institutional investors (March 31, June 30, September 30 and December 31).

TABLE 7.2   Summer Rally (Dow Jones Industrial Average)

Year	% Change, June–August
1947	+0.5%
1948	−4.7
1949	+7.5
1950	+4.7
1951	+11.8
1952	−0.1
1953	−4.1
1954	+2.1
1955	+5.7
1956	+1.3
1957	−4.6
1958	+6.0
1959	+3.4
1960	−0.3
1961	+4.9
1962	+8.0
1963	+4.6
1964	+1.3
1965	+3.7
1966	−9.1
1967	+3.5
1968	−0.6
1969	−2.4
1970	+11.3
1971	+3.5
1972	+2.6
1973	−4.7
1974	−15.3
1975	+0.1
1976	−17.4

SOURCE: C. Colburn Hardy, *Your Investments*, 1977–1978 ed. (New York: Thomas Y. Crowell, 1977).

These are the weeks to garner quick profits by acquiring institutionally favored stocks which have had a big move in the last few months. Aggressive money managers add to their winning holdings to improve their reported performance. Their heavy buying can push prices up several points.

Within any month. Sell during the first five trading days. For the past quarter of a century, this has been profitable about two-thirds of the time. The reason: Many individuals and most institutions operate on a monthly basis. They make their decisions soon after the end of the month and start buying promptly. Demand exceeds supply and prices move higher.

Within any week. Buy Monday morning and sell Friday afternoon. Over a 42-year period, Arthur A. Merrill found that the DJIA went down 54% of the Mondays and up on 63% of the Fridays.

This was confirmed by another study which showed that, at Friday's close, the market averaged 0.12% higher than the Thursday's final and 0.22% above the Monday's last price.[2]

Unless you are trading in large lots, the differences may be small; but every extra dollar counts.

Within any day. The first and last hours of any day are likely to be the most active. The opening hour volume is boosted by overnight decisions, and many traders review the market at 2 PM and make their moves before closing.

High volume in the morning can be a yellow light. When the first hour trading tops 8.5 million shares, the DJIA is likely to be down 10–20 points within the next 24 hours.

In the last hour, prices tend to decline as professionals take their daily profits or losses.

Before holidays. The market tends to rise about 66% of the time prior to a one-day respite and 75% before a three-day break.

OTHER FORECASTING TOOLS

Here again, the guides/statistics/ratios are legion. Some are too complex to be computed easily, but others are available in publications or printed services. These are typical:

Utility stocks. This is a group which often moves before the overall market. Stocks of electrical and gas companies are supersensitive to interest rates. The companies are large borrowers and their shares are bought

---

[2]Arthur A. Merrill, Chappaqua, N.Y., letter to C. Colburn Hardy, February 28, 1977.

primarily for yield rather than for growth. Utilities are the first choice for conservative investors when they move out of bonds into common stocks.

The best guide is the Dow Jones Utility Average (DJUA) (Chart 7.1). Here's how some of its forecasts fared:

- In April 1965 the DJUA topped out before the DJIA, which reached its peak in February 1966. Later that year, the utilities bottomed out before the industrials.
- In 1968 the utilities moved ahead of the industrials again, but in 1970 came the exception that proved the rule: The DJUA bottomed *after* the DJIA.
- In 1972 the old pattern held: In June the utilities hit a low before the industrials and, in November, reached a high, two months before the DJIA scored its record peak.
- In 1975 the forecast was correct. After an early rise, the DJUA wavered, then moved up throughout 1976. The DJIA fell in the fall of 1975 and, as signaled, recovered by year's end.

Mutual fund liquidity. Indicators like this are often used by chartists as background. This shows the percentage of cash and liquid assets to total assets of major investment companies. Usually, this ranges between 4.5% and 6.5%.

As guidelines, many technicians sell when the liquidity drops below 5% and consider buying when it moves above 6.5%. The reason: Investment companies tend to be more liquid when the market is ready to go up and to be fully invested when stocks are near a peak.

Caveat: This indicator may be useful in normal markets but is of questionable worth in deep bear markets such as in 1969–1970, when money managers became wary of stocks. What's more, in recent years, heavy net redemptions have kept mutual funds scrambling for cash and, therefore, have distorted this indicator.

Credit balances with brokers. This is similar to Mutual Fund Liquidity but refers to cash left by individuals with brokers. It's best as a negative market indicator. When it's high, investors are pessimistic and unwilling to take extra risks.

Like many specialized forecasting tools, this indicator can involve complex calculations. Martin E. Zweig, a leading technician, uses these signals to time selling:

- Credit balances are up for four consecutive months, then contract three times, by a minimum of 10%;
- Credit balances rise 30% in four of five months, then decline, by at least 10%, for four straight months;

Chart 7.1 36-YEAR PANORAMA OF INVESTMENT MARKETS

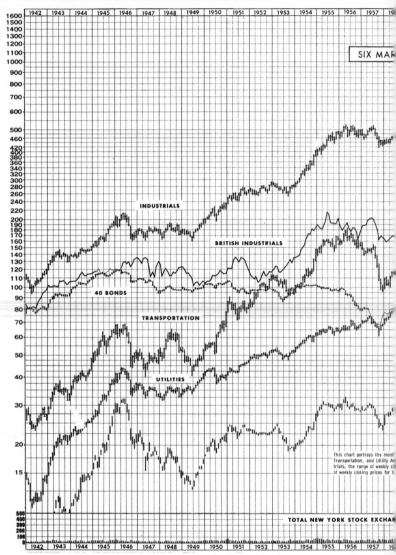

SOURCE: Trendline, Inc.

Sell on the tenth business day following the last monthly data. This allows for the delay in the release of the information.

Well, that's what the man said in *Barron's!*[3]

Interest rates. This is a device used to predict market swings and prices of

[3]Martin E. Zweig, *Barron's*, January 20, 1975 (digested).

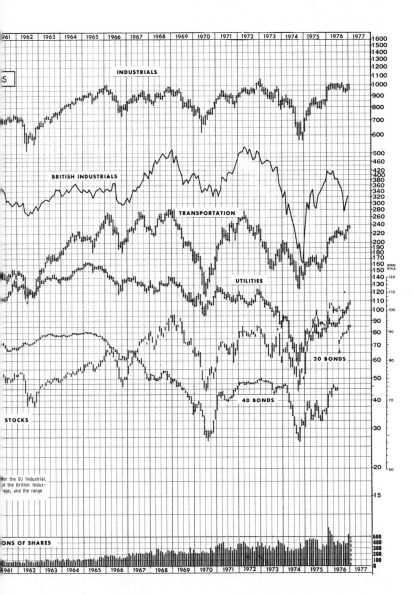

individual stocks on the basis of shifts in interest rates. Donald C. DeLutis of John Nuveen & Co. relates the cost of money to the price/earnings ratio to project a stock's price; i.e., when the interest rate is around 7%, Texaco is worth 11.5 times its previous 12-month profits; with money at 7.5%, the stock measurement is a multiple of 11, etc.

For his interest rate figure, DeLutis calculates an average of AAA-rated corporate, utility and telephone bonds. He then multiplies the multiple of all DJIA stocks to estimate where the Dow should go.

Over nine years, 27 of the 32 projections were correct. This is, of course, a refinement of the established fact that values of stocks are strongly influenced by shifts in the interest rate.

Some of these indicators may seem esoteric and an exercise in the technician's ego, but basically, they all rely on the technical theory that what has happened before will happen again—with the stock market generally and with stock groups specifically. Most of these forecasters provide useful and generally accurate background for trading and investment decisions. *But never buy or sell on the predictions of technical indicators by themselves. Look for consensus and confirmation.*

SHORT INTEREST: A HANDY PREDICTOR

When a stock is sold short, it usually means that the seller is pessimistic and expects to be able to buy back the shares at a lower price in the not too distant future. But with its usual optimism and delight in contrary opinion, Wall Street takes the view that a large short position is bullish and a small one bearish.

This conclusion is based on the fact that most short sales are made with borrowed stocks, and since these shares will have to be bought eventually, the bigger the short position, the greater the ultimate demand and the higher the market and the prices of shorted stocks. Maybe so. But as long as the price falls, there is little incentive to buy. When there is a reversal, short coverings will accentuate the buying pressure. But it is not the short interest, as such, which causes the turnaround.

Whatever the validity of this theory, short sales are a favorite technical indicator. They provide a continuing yardstick of market pessimism. They are valuable in pinpointing the end of a bear cycle or the inception of a new bull market. They are not overly effective in forecasting the end of bull markets or of bull market movements.

To technicians, short positions are relative: An active market can support relatively high short positions without being technically bullish; in an active market, an average short position may be bullish. All of which points out that short interest indicators should be used in conjunction with, and after confirmation by, other signals. About the only thing that is sure is that short sales almost always move opposite to the market: *up* as the DJIA goes *down*, and *down* as the DJIA goes *up*.

Using Short Interest and Ratios

There are several major short interest indicators and ratios used in calculations.

Short Interest Each time a stock listed on the NYSE or AMEX is sold short, the transaction is recorded and the accumulation is reported—daily by the number of odd lot shares and monthly four business days after the 15th of the following month. The monthly data show totals of the exchange and of shares of specific companies with comparisons to the previous month of (1) short positions of 20,000 shares, and (2) changes, in the short position of the previous month, of at least 10,000 shares. Table 7.3 shows the start of a table of the NYSE.

As of February 15, 1977, the total short interest on the Big Board was 26,261,329 shares, down from January's total of 26,873,693. The average January daily trading volume was 24,000,049, down from 24,086,857.

To calculate the Short Interest Ratio (SIR), divide that average daily volume into the monthly short interest: 1.09 and 1.12, respectively.

TABLE 7.3   Short Position: New York Stock Exchange

	2-15-77	1-14-77	Average daily volume
AMF Inc	33,900	17,200	39,157
ASA Ltd	154,846	181,161	17,452
Aetna Life Casualty	21,550	43,150	81,533
Air Products & Chem	55,940	41,404	37,714
Alco Standard Corp	17,922	5,366	9,652
Allied Chemical Corp	64,260	68,560	53,742
Allis-Chalmers Corp	50,510	9,460	19,247
Aluminum Co America	28,425	74,550	41,347
tAmax Inc	179,700	172,463	16,909
Amax Inc sr B cv pr	14,116	None	2,757
tAmerada Hess Corp	382,134	149,888	124,528
Amer Airlines	9,193	37,338	33,285
Amer Broadcasting Co	89,471	90,020	42,266
Amer Cyanamid Co	18,322	80,210	34,419
Amer Electric Power	13,860	56,883	45,676
Amer General Ins Co	69,032	124,269	18,752
Amer Home Products	25,492	9,082	79,376
Amer Hospital Supply	94,292	173,692	41,419
Amer Motors Corp	74,667	72,667	32,304

NOTE: t = possibly involved in arbitrage depending on prices of securities involved. Thus, not always true short sales.

SOURCE: New York Stock Exchange. For the period ending February 15, 1977, as reported in *The Wall Street Journal*.

As a rule of thumb, an SIR of 2.0 or more is very bullish; at 1.5 to 2.0, bullish; 1.0 to 1.5, neutral; below 1.0, bearish.

Take these with a grain of salt:

- The short interest tends to decline from December to January because many investors with good profits, which they prefer not to take for tax reasons, sell shares short against the box, i.e., not by borrowing but against shares they own. They want to transfer their profits to the next year and, usually, cover their positions in January. They are long and short at the same time, so that month's SIR is not as reliable as it is later in the year.

- Short positions are most valuable in spotting volatile stocks, that is, those more likely to rise or fall rapidly in a few weeks or months.

- Always use SIR in conjunction with Specialists Short Sales, which, at extremes, can cancel out technical interpretations and flash opposite signals.

If you believe that stocks will rise in the near future, take a look at stocks with the highest short interest. You will get more bang for your buck.

Conversely, if you are bearish, do not short stocks with high short interest. A market rally may force their prices to rise and you'll be in trouble.

Odd Lot Short Sales   According to Wall Street wisdom, odd lotters are the most consistently incorrect of all speculators. When they indicate greater pessimism by increasing the number of short sales (when the odd lot sales ratio moves to high levels), the market is likely to prove them wrong by staging a rise.

Here again, the ratio is the technical indicator. This is calculated by dividing the odd lot short sales by the total odd lot sales. To catch the trend, most technicians translate this into a moving average.

Here's an example from The Professional Tape Reader:[4]

Customer Purchases	Short Sales	Other Sales	Total Sales
130,392	1,828	363,907	365,735

Odd Lot Short Sales Ratio (OLSSR): 1,828   363,907 = 0.50

According to a study by *Barron's*, this is a reliable indicator. The higher the ratio, the greater the market rise over the next 30 days and the higher the average percent change.

---

[4]Stan Weinstein, The Professional Tape Reader, New York, in confirmation letter to C. Colburn Hardy, March 1, 1977.

Of 65 times when the OLSSR fell to between 3.0 and 4.0, the market rose almost 68% of the time. The best results were predicted at the ratio highs: When over 6.0, the future market was higher in the next 30 days 96% of the time. *Conclusion:* When the OLSSR is over 4.0, the chances are 75% that the market will be higher in the next month. When it's over 5.0, the chances of a rise are 90%.

At the time of this calculation, the signal was very bearish. It was correct: The market fell sharply.

Specialist Short Selling Ratio (SSSR)   This is based on the short selling done by specialists on the floor of the exchange. The ratio is calculated by dividing the number of shares shorted by these professionals in a given week by the total number of shares sold short by everyone. The statistics are available on Monday in *Barron's* and *The Wall Street Journal*. Because of the time needed for tabulation, the figures lag two weeks behind the actual transactions.

When the ratio drops to 40% or less, it's a bullish alert; near 65%, it's a bearish forecast.

This indicator has an excellent record of calling major turns in the market. It should be used in connection with other short interest ratios because, at extremes, it can cancel out other technical interpretations and flash opposite signals.

If you have to choose between these short interest ratios, stick with SSSR. This shows what the experts have been doing, and since short selling is the way they make their living, they don't make many mistakes.

LONDON STOCK MARKET INDEX

One of the most useful technical forecasters is the London Financial Times Index. This is sort of a Dow Jones Industrial Average for the London Stock Exchange. It is a favorite tool for some of the most successful professional money managers.

The daily U.S. financial press lists the averages of 30 stocks and of 500 stocks as traded the previous day. The Dow Jones ticker reports the opening figures early each business morning. (Remember, London is three hours ahead of New York.)

The easiest way to use this forecaster on a continuing basis is to plot trendlines on the quarterly chart which shows the long-term data of both the London and New York Stock Exchanges (available from Securities Research Company; see References).

Generally, the London index will lead the NYSE by one to two weeks, but occasionally, the time span will be longer, especially when the pound is in trouble. To technicians, the significance of this foreign index is that the financial world is international. They know that what happens with stocks of Beecham Group, British-American Tobacco, Imperial Chemical Industries and other worldwide companies presages activity in shares of U.S. corporations. Today most professional money managers take a global view of their investments.

Aid to Timing

Richard Blackman, a successful trader, feels that the London Index is a 90% correct leading indicator. He uses it primarily as a traffic signal. He seldom buys until the British market is positive and usually sells or stays out of the market when it's negative.[5]

Here are some examples of how the London Index forecast moves on the American market:

December 1956—London bottomed at 170. Two weeks later, the Dow fell to 455.

April 1957—London peaked at 210. Within weeks, the Dow started up and hit a new high of 520 in June.

Spring 1962—London fell to 252. The Dow was close behind, with a low of 524.

October 1966—London dropped to 284. The Dow, after a sharp spurt, declined to 735.

October 1968—London soared to 521, a few weeks before the Dow jumped to 994.

April 1970—London fell to 315. A month later, the Dow was down to 627.

Fall 1974—London was down to 144, signaling the Dow dive to 570.

January 1976—London moved to 418 from a low of 146 the year before. In March the Dow hit 1012.

To get an edge on the market, watch the London Index and use its trends in planning trading tactics. It can be most useful in helping you to get into profitable situations early and to get out of or avoid money-losing decisions.

---

[5]Personal interview with Richard Blackman, manager of Paramus, N.J., office of Herzfeld and Stern, in October 1976.

EIGHT

Channels, Support and Resistance Levels and Consolidation Areas

Closely related to trendlines are other drawn-in configurations such as channels, support and resistance levels and consolidation areas. They are cited frequently by analysts to explain what these technicians think is happening in the marketplace. They are better-suited for conversation, market letters and obfuscation than for use. For most people, trendlines are the best, the easiest to use and the most reliable of all such technical indicators.

Channels are an extension of trendlines. They are more of a convenience than a necessity, are not overly reliable and are much more valuable for traders than investors. They can be formed after a trend has been established by connecting the last two or three high points with a straight line. (See Chart 8.1.) Generally, they parallel the trendline.

As long as the stock moves with the two lines, traders will buy when the stock is at the bottom of the channel and sell at the top for a few points' profit. These speculators know that until one of the lines is clearly penetrated, the up-and-down movement will probably be repeated.

With Tandy, in the fall of 1976, the trader might start to buy at 32, sell at

38, wait a bit and buy again at 37, sell at 42, etc. As long as the trendline is up and is not penetrated, the trader will continue to profit.

Similarly, a trader might have sold short at around 44 in early 1976, covered at 36, sold short at 40, covered at 33 and stopped completely when the upside breakout came in June.

When the top of the channel is penetrated, it's a new ball game. Basically, this is a sell signal but, as outlined later, may be a time to buy or add to present holdings. The important line is still the bottom trendline, because it is the base from which advances are made, toward which declines return and below which sales should be made.

When you draw channels, make the bottom uptrendline as tight as possible. This is your buy point. In trading, the top line marks the sell point. Cyclical stocks will move within a channel for three to six months. Always be sure that the latest channel corresponds to the historical width. Aberrations of a point or two indicate changes which could be costly.

If the tops are so erratic that you cannot project the channel, draw a line connecting the bottoms and then pencil in a parallel line at the same distance as that of the historical channel: i.e., if the long-term chart shows a four-square (¼ inch) swing, draw the top line four squares above the base trendline.

The value of a channel for traders is that it sets limits: Buy at the bottom and sell at the top. If you are an optimist, you may want to be a bit more daring. Buy at just under the trendline on what appears to be the start of an upmove and sell just above the top channel line. Do this only in a strong bull market.

Chart 8.1   CHANNELS

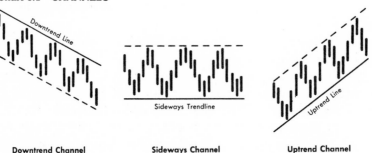

| Downtrend Channel | Sideways Channel | Uptrend Channel |

SOURCE: William L. Jiler, *How Charts Can Help You in the Stock Market* (New York: Trendline, Inc., 1972).

Chart 8.2   SUPPORT LEVELS

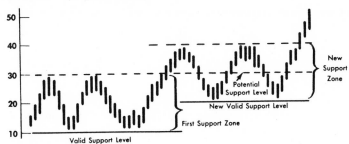

SOURCE: William L. Jiler, *How Charts Can Help You in the Stock Market* (New York: Trendline, Inc., 1972).

SUPPORT AND RESISTANCE LEVELS

Support and resistance levels are created by previous trading and investment commitments. They involve both price and volume and usually indicate areas where it pays to make decisions.

Support is the price level where a declining security may be expected to be supported by buyers. It's usually the area of acquisition before the price rise.

Resistance is the price level where an advancing security may be expected to be dumped by sellers.

Support Level

Many technicians use these patterns for projections rather than for completing full charts. They draw a straight line to connect the bottoms and a dotted line to indicate the top. In between are the vertical movements made up of a series of fluctuations within a fairly narrow range, say 5 points, with a top of 30 and a bottom of 25. When the stock falls to 25, chances are it will work its way back to 30 and, if the overall market is good and the stock is becoming popular, build a new support level at 27. In the next support pattern, the high might be 32, etc. In a strong market, this could form the base for a further advance.

Generally, the pattern is reversed with a down stock. This is the time to be pessimistic. It takes a lot more investor interest to reverse a decline than to spur an upmove.

Forget about the *why* of the stock action. When the chart shows a support level, wait to be sure that it holds and then start buying and looking for the breakout into a new high.

As a general rule, this pattern follows that of the sketch: an upmove, a dip, a second move to about the same height as before, another drop to what is now becoming the support level and, on the third rise, the breakout.

From the new high, the stock will probably retrace about half its gain. A new support level will form, often under the 50% rule, at the midpoint of the original channel.

Watch the volume. If the upmove is with heavier trading, the advance will probably be strong and fast *if* the overall market is favorable.

As shown by Chart 8.2, the support zone forms a channel and thus the basis for trading. Speculators would buy on the first upmove, sell at the reversal point, buy back at the support level and then wait, hoping for the breakout.

Caveat: In real life, the support levels and patterns are not quite so easy to identify, but with weekly and, occasionally, monthly charts, they can be identified. There is one convenient alternative: trendlines. These can be drawn between the low points of the upmove and used as signals to buy when the uptrend is confirmed, to sell on the reversal, to buy back again on the second rise and to hold into the new high ground.

For both investors and traders, support levels are most valuable as a base. As always, the overall market trend is very important. A strong stock may find support in a slightly down market, but only rarely will there be significant upmoves until the averages rise.

For profits and protection, set your target prices before you buy and never hesitate to sell when there's a confirmed break down through the previous support level.

Resistance Levels

Resistance levels are the opposite of support areas. They are the points where the selling, actual or potential, is enough to satisfy all bids and stop prices from going higher. If a stock moves up and down for some time at a level which is only slightly higher than has been reached in the past, the odds are high that resistance is formidable and there will be a downside break.

On the other hand, if the stock move penetrates the top level, it may be a signal for investors to buy and short sellers to cover. The old resistance level will become a support area. This indicates a shift in supply and demand. Buyers outnumber sellers and are willing to pay ever higher prices.

Example: A stock drops from 70 to 50 in a selling climax. Then it jumps a few points with little volume. Then it falls back to 42. As it moves up again, it will probably encounter resistance at 50. This is the price where buyers, mindful of the 70 high, thought they were getting a bargain. They want to get out even. If the stock falls again to, say, 45, and then recovers, that 50 will continue to be a resistance level until the supply dries up.

The pattern of resistance levels varies with the price of the stock. Buyers of low-priced issues, say at 5, will accept a decline to 3½, even though this is a 30% loss. But buyers of higher-priced stocks, say at 50, will start bailing out at 45, a 10% loss.

Both support and resistance levels represent reversals of recent trends. The best way to judge future action is by a look at the historical pattern of the stocks as shown on charts. Look for the areas where there is power (volume potential) to move the stock in the direction you want. Pay special attention to the trading pattern at similar price levels of the past. In the Dow Chemical chart, the resistance points were 34, the new high, followed by dips until the resistance was finally overcome, and for the future, 56, the record high.

Once a stock moves back to a previous peak, there is sure to be selling. If the volume is heavy, as with Dow in late August 1973, the latent demand may be depleted quickly. On the other hand, if there's a sharp rise—penetration of the resistance area, as in 1975—the heavy volume may signal a true breakout. With Dow, this was temporary because of the possibility of a stock split. Once this was completed, the trend reversed.

Chart 8.3   OLD RESISTANCE BECOMES NEW SUPPORT

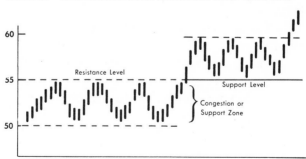

SOURCE: William L. Jiler, *How Charts Can Help You in the Stock Market* (New York: Trendline, Inc., 1972).

The toughest decision is to determine whether a move out of the support or resistance area is significant. Will the trend continue or will there be a pullback and establishment of a new area? It's easy to guess wrong, so you must check daily.

Remember, you are always competing with some tough-minded traders. At any support level, there are vested interests who see this as a point to cash in or to switch. With resistance levels, their decisions will be reversed.

Example: A stock scores a new high at 62, then falls back to 57 and jumps to 68. Says John Magee, "Many traders will see 57 as the support level but it's more likely to be 62. Those who wanted to buy at 57 but hesitated, may not wait until the stock drops to the old low. They will regard 62 as a bargain price."[1]

Magee believes that "with both support and resistance levels, there are no surefire formulas. You must use judgment based on volume, the time the stocks stay within the area and on overall market conditions. Usually, people underestimate the amount of resistance. Since you feel bullish, you assume that others do, too. This may not be true."[2]

One way to guess the real resistance level is to average the closing prices for the days making up the bottom congestion. Vice versa for support. The results will come close to the center of gravity.

Guidelines for Using Support and Resistance Levels

- Use daily or weekly charts to catch developments and longer-term charts for determining key points.
- Consider a bottom support more valid than a top one.
- Keep checking support levels to see if the stock stays on course. As long as the support holds, the stock is doing well and you can buy more shares.
- Buy when the stock returns to its support level after a temporary rise, if you are convinced of the merits and prospects of the company.
- Sell when the stock hits and stays at a resistance level.
- Sell when a stock falls through a support base.
- Act on a confirmed breakout of either support or resistance levels: Buy on the upside and sell on the downside. But be sure the potential gains are worthwhile. Commissions can take a big bite out of short-term profits.

[1]John Magee, *Technical Analysis of Stock Trends* (John Magee: Springfield, Mass., 1975) p. 213.
[2]Ibid.

CONSOLIDATION AREAS

These are closely related to support and resistance levels. They occur when a stock has moved up or down too fast, reaches a point of exhaustion, reverses a bit and then settles down within a narrow range.

On the chart, this shows up as a series of minor fluctuations—sort of a combination of both support and resistance levels.

Consolidation areas are significant when they are not typical of the historical stock action. With Libbey-Owens-Ford Co. (LOF), the long-term chart (Chart 8.4) shows wide, fairly frequent swings, a V formation with a sharp rise and then the consolidation. It's more apparent on the short-term chart (Chart 8.5): After a long period of meandering between 30 and 34, LOF broke up to 37, and then consolidated again at a higher level in December and January.

Consolidation patterns are frequent with stable, slow-growth stocks such as those of utilities. They are worth watching (and then not too closely)

Chart 8.4   CONSOLIDATION AREAS: LONG TERM

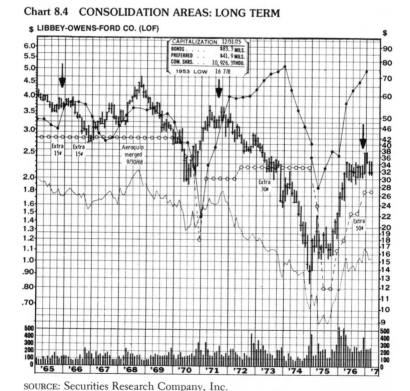

SOURCE: Securities Research Company, Inc.

Chart 8.5 CONSOLIDATION AREAS: SHORT TERM

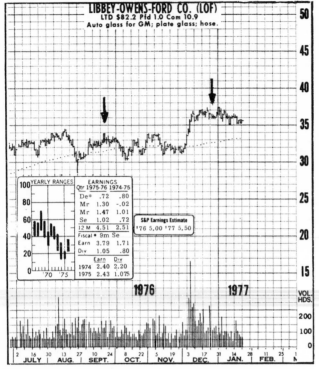

SOURCE: Trendline, Inc.

with quality stocks which, by fundamental analysis, are still undervalued. The narrow price range indicates that investors can't make up their minds. Eventually, some major holders will act, as with LOF in early December when the stock zoomed with extraordinarily heavy volume.

It's difficult to predict the ultimate direction of a breakout, but generally, it will follow the trend just prior and be in tune with the overall market.

The trouble with consolidation patterns is that you can't make money. The stock is just marking time. If you own the stock and are optimistic, hold on and hope. But do not buy any stock in a consolidation pattern until there's a favorable upmove or, if you're a short seller, you expect unfavorable news or action.

Perhaps the best explanation of the value of a consolidation pattern came from a Wall Street veteran: "Consolidation is an excuse made by a security analyst who predicted the stock would move up but now finds it's going nowhere."

NINE

Checking the Financial Pages

The financial pages of *The Wall Street Journal* and major daily newspapers carry a wealth of information which can be used for technical analysis. Similar data is also available in *Barron's*, *Commercial and Financial Chronicle* and *The Financial Weekly*.

These report the market action of the previous day or week. They are very important for monitoring trends, finding unusual opportunities and getting a feel of the market. Always review them before you check your charts.

You will find many more tables than are explained here. As you become more knowledgeable, you may want to add other data. There's no place in the business world where more information is presented so frequently as in Wall Street. Take advantage of these facts to improve your investment/trading skills.

MOST ACTIVE STOCKS: WHAT
MAJOR INVESTORS ARE BUYING
AND SELLING

Each day, the financial press lists the Most Active stocks: 15 for the NYSE and 10 each for the ASE and OTC (Table 9.1). Similar data, also based on

TABLE 9.1   NYSE Most Active Stocks

Name	Volume	Last	Net change
AmAirlin	285,600	11¾	−¼
AmTel& Tel	207,100	63¾	+⅝
GenMotors	163,900	70½	+¾
Royalwduf	150,000	54⅝	. . . .
EastKodak	149,300	72¾	+1½
BritPet	148,400	15½	−½
GlfWindwt	144,600	1⅝	. . . .
DowCh	140,300	36¾	. . . .
CoastStGas	134,900	15⅛	−¼
KresgeSS	134,300	35¼	+⅝
Exxon	127,400	52¼	+½
AmHospit	124,300	26⅛	−¼
SearsRoeb	123,800	62½	+⅛
TexacoInd	123,500	27⅞	+¼
CaterpTr	123,400	49⅞	. . . .

SOURCE: New York Stock Exchange for Monday, February 14, 1977, as reported in *The New York Times*.

the volume of shares traded, are reported weekly: in *Barron's* for 20 stocks on the NYSE and 10 for the other markets, and in *The Financial Weekly* for 40 leaders for the three major markets.

Usually, about half the names will be those of huge corporations with hundreds of millions of shares, such as AT&T, GM and Exxon. The stocks to watch, however, are the newcomers—familiar corporations with relatively limited capitalization. Their names and their industry group tell where the action is, and their action tells a lot about the market.

These Most Active stocks represent only about 1% of the total number of issues traded, but their volume represents 10% to 15% of overall activity. The price trends of those popular (or unpopular) stocks can be an excellent guide to the direction of the NYSE, especially when considered in relation to stock market averages. Generally, these leaders are stronger than the market in upswings and weaker in downswings.

One week's data are meaningless, but three weeks can be a good base for investment decisions: generally for the trend of the overall market; specifically for the future action of individual stocks.

Making Your Own Index

To make use of these indicators, many technicians compute a Most Active Moving Average Index. To do this on a daily basis, set down the net difference between the number of stocks which went up and the number which went down. Thus, if there were 12 advances and 3 declines, the net is +9. The next day, 10 are up, 4 are down and one is unchanged, so this net is +6.

Add the 30-day total and divide by 30 to get the Most Active Moving Average (MA). Then, on the 31st day, remove the oldest data and add the newest and so on.

As a general rule, it's buying time when the net indicator is +3 or higher, and a sell signal when it's −3 or lower. But as with all technical indicators, the decision should be made only after reviewing other guidelines.

Value of Most Active Stocks

Technicians use these lists of Most Active stocks for the following reasons:

1. *To discover when new industry groups are coming in or out of favor.* When two or three stocks of the same industry group—chemicals, office equipment, utilities, etc.—appear on the list for a week, check back and hold the clipping for future review. If this pattern covers at least three weeks, it's a good indication of investor sentiment. If all these stocks show higher closing prices, turn to the charts, first of the group and then of the individual companies. Draw the trendlines to find the direction of their movement, and get ready to act on this information.

2. *To spot new profit opportunities (stocks to buy in up markets and stocks to sell short in down markets).* This review goes hand in hand with step 1. If the group or market actions are favorable, one or more of these Most Actives may be ready for a big move. This is the time to bring in every tool of technical analysis.

Example: In September 1976, ITT (Chart 9.1) appeared on the Most Active list for several, almost consecutive, weeks. The stock was selling at about 32. A check of the conglomerate group showed favorable movement. The fundamentals were also good: strong financial base, improving earnings and expansion into new, growing markets. ITT was a candidate for trading and, possibly, investment profits.

Wise technicians waited for confirmation. They started to buy when the market—and ITT—dipped, or when the stock appeared again on the Most Active list. This was proof that some institutions were still in a buying mood.

Nothing happened until late November when, despite a generally flat market, ITT moved up, slowly and with heavy volume, to 34.

In December the stock dipped a bit but, in January, continued strong despite the market fluctuations. Late in the month, as shown by the list, the stock moved to 34⅜, a new three-year high. Early buyers had a 10%

Chart 9.1 FOLLOWING MOST ACTIVE STOCKS: LONG TERM

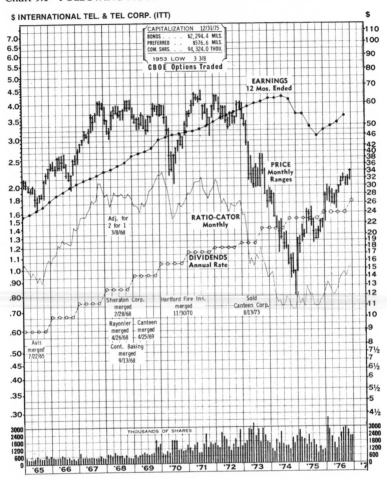

SOURCE: Securities Research Company, Inc.

profit and looked for further gains. By watching the Most Active list, they spotted a potential winner. Sad to say, the overall market went down, so only shrewd traders made money. But ITT held fairly well.

The reverse occurs in a bear market. Heavily traded stocks with ever lower prices are the best stocks to short. These are the issues which major investors want to sell. And when these professionals make up their mind to get out of a stock, they seldom care what price they get. As a result, these Most Active stocks will decline fast and far—the ideal situation for short selling.

For Traders Only

The Most Active list is also a hunting ground for traders looking for quick profits, especially in secondary stocks. This is what happened with Milgo Electronics when 266,100 shares were traded with a 6-point jump.

Milgo is a small electronics firm which, at the time, was a target for acquisition and had received several increasingly higher offers. The trading volume represented about 20% of its total shares, and the 27⅝ price was almost double the share value when the company listed on the NYSE six months before.

Chart 9.2 FOLLOWING MOST ACTIVE STOCKS: SHORT TERM

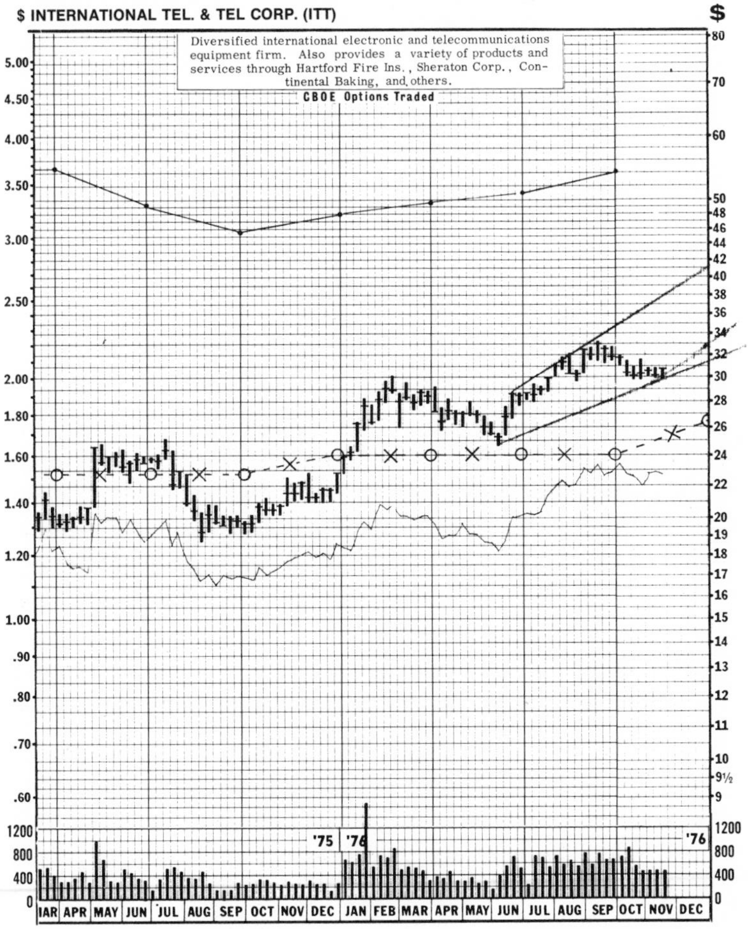
$ INTERNATIONAL TEL. & TEL CORP. (ITT)
$
Diversified international electronic and telecommunications equipment firm. Also provides a variety of products and services through Hartford Fire Ins., Sheraton Corp., Continental Baking, and others.
CBOE Options Traded
'75 '76
'76
IAR APR MAY JUN JUL AUG SEP OCT NOV DEC JAN FEB MAR APR MAY JUN JUL AUG SEP OCT NOV DEC

SOURCE: Securities Research Company, Inc.

Whether the trader bought long or sold short depended on the circumstances. Either way, a quick profit was sought on the basis of the extraordinary interest.

The sellers were shrewd speculators who had watched the chart and bought the stock the previous November when it moved to around 20 with extra-high volume.

The buyers, in part, were arbitrageurs betting that a takeover would be completed by Applied Digital Data Systems through a new class of preferred stock valued at $32 per share.

Always keep an eye on the Most Active stocks, but before you act on this information, check other technical and fundamental factors. This list is most valuable as a billboard to advertise investor stocks which are either in or out of favor of institutional holders.

ADVANCE/DECLINE (A/D) LINE

This is an easy-to-plot and easy-to-watch indicator, because the basic data is published daily. On a chart, a line is drawn from the tabulation of the cumulative totals of daily advances and declines of NYSE stocks. This can cover any length of time but is used most frequently for 10 days and 200 days.

The A/D line does not show exactly when a rally or reaction will occur but only that it will come soon. Most technicians regard it as more significant than the DJIA and believe that it shows clearly what the market is doing and gives a strong signal of what it will do. It works best when confirmed by other indicators, but almost always reveals a trend which, it's worth repeating, remains intact until there's a definite reversal.

Table 9.2 gives the basic data for plotting a 10-day A/D line in early 1977.

Using A/D Line

This indicator can be used directly, as a ratio or in comparison with a market average. Rules on profitable interpretation are explained here.

Directly In a bull market, a bearish signal is flashed when:
- The A/D line slopes down at the same time the market average is rising.
- The 200-day total of net advances and declines falls from a peak toward a minus position.

In a bull market, a bullish signal is flashed when:
- The A/D line swings up, dips and then recovers to a new high.

TABLE 9.2 *Advance/Decline Data*

Day	Advances	Declines	Cumulative advances	Cumulative declines	Cumulative difference	DJIA
1	735	693	735	693	+42	946.31
2	671	737	1406	1430	−24	942.24
3	405	1029	1811	2459	−648	933.84
4	728	722	2539	3181	−642	937.92
5	540	864	3079	4045	−966	931.52
6	738	701	3817	4746	−929	938.33
7	840	602	4657	5348	−691	944.32
8	884	572	5541	5920	−379	948.30
9	480	918	6021	6838	−817	943.73
10	573	798	6594	7636	−1042	940.24
11	670	780	7264	8416	−1152	939.91

SOURCE: New York Stock Exchange as reported in *The New York Times*, February 1977.

In a bear market, a bullish signal is flashed when:

- The A/D line declines, rallies and then declines below the previous low.
- The 200-day total moves up from negative and climbs above zero to plus figures.

As a Ratio   As calculated by technician Harvey A. Krow, this is the result of dividing the advances by the declines. Any answer greater than 1.00 would show advances exceeding declines. All numbers from 0.99 down indicate more declines than advances.[1]

When using this indicator, study the relationship of the curves or, if you prefer numbers, multiply the ratio by 100 to express the result in percentages. Thus, if the ratio were 1.05, it would mean that the number of advancing stocks was 105% of the number declining. On balance, the market would be moving up 5%.

Here's how the ratio would look with the calculations based on continuing the first example:

Day	Advances	10-Day moving total	Declines	10-Day moving total	Ratio of moving advances to moving declines
11	670	7264	780	8416	.86
12	609	7873	796	9212	.85
13	459	8332	992	10204	.82
14	555	8887	841	11045	.82

[1]Harvey A. Krow, *Stock Market Behavior* (New York: Random House, 1969), confirmed with personal conversation with C. Colburn Hardy, March 1977.

The 10-day ratio:

- An advance of 0.05 after a decline to less than 0.50 is a bullish signal in a bear market. Usually, there will be two or more of these climatic dumpings of securities.
- A decline below 0.75 signals a short-term buying opportunity, almost always in bull markets and usually during the intermediate rally in the early stages of a bear market.
- A decline below 0.50 occurs most frequently in the late stages of a bear market.
- A rise above 1.25 creates a selling opportunity, except in the first stages of a bull market.
- The failure to rise above 1.40 after a fall to 0.65 suggests that the rally is likely to be abortive.
- A rise above 1.40 implies the probability of at least two more uplegs in the market.

In Comparison with a Market Average   When the DJIA is used for comparison, the strength of the movement is indicated by how much and how long the price average differs from the A/D line.

The market will turn up when:

- The DJIA falls while the A/D rises.
- The DJIA nears a previous low and the A/D line is well above where it was when the low was made.

The market will go down when:

- The DJIA rises while the A/D falls.
- The DJIA moves near a previous top and the A/D stays below the reading which corresponds to that top.

In addition, of course, the A/D figures report the progress of the overall market. With the figures cited above, the market was declining and showed no sign of reversing. The indicator was accurate. The market continued down for several months.

HIGHS AND LOWS

These daily figures for NYSE stocks are more psychological than useful. Investors tend to be confident when more stocks touch new highs than new lows and bearish when the reverse is true. But this popular index of the market's well-being is not always on target. The base is changed on March 15 of each year. Before that date, the comparisons are made with figures including prices of the past year. After the 15th of March, the reference points are the quotations of the current year: 2½ months only.

This list can provide leads to potential winners and does spotlight group activity; and when it includes stocks you hold, it can make you feel better (or worse). But most of the time, the names are those of smaller corporations whose stocks are of little interest to major investors, preferred stocks whose prices reflect interest rates more than supply and demand and issues which a smart technician should have been watching anyway. By the time a quality stock is listed in the Highs and Lows, you should have caught the signals from your charts and either be ready to take profits or consider a sale at a quick, small loss.

TEN

Moving Averages for Signals, Evaluation and Trading

A moving average (MA) is a mathematical device for smoothing out a series of fluctuating values over a period of time. It is formed by adding a specific number of prices (of a market average, a stock group or an individual issue) and dividing the total by the number of entries. As each new unit is added, the first is deleted. This causes a price change, hence the term "moving average."

Most technicians plot the data on a chart to provide a trend measurement.

Table 10.1 shows a comparison of the DJIA and ITT stock.

At the end of day 10, the total for the DJIA is 9,624.30, or when divided by 10, an MA of 962.43. On the 11th day, add 963.60 and drop the 986.87, etc.

With ITT, the 11th day rise to a new high of 34⅜ is added and the first entry, 34, is deleted.

A chart will show the relationship more clearly, but the numbers indicate that the stock has performed better than the overall market index: Its declines were less, its gains greater and its action was more stable than that of the Dow. The trend of the stock is favorable.

The length of an MA depends on the investment objective. Traders prefer 3, 10 or 30 days; investors like a longer period of 60, 100 or 200 days; and managers of pension and profit-sharing funds often use three years.

USES OF THE MA

MAs are an integral part of technical analysis of the market and individual stocks. They have two general uses: to spot trends and thus aid timing, and to measure investment performance. They are most valuable when used in comparisons: for example, an individual stock or portfolio versus a group or stock market average.

On the same chart, the technician plots the MAs of both and then looks for comparative trends. With a stock and the DJIA, the technician would watch for these signals:

■ As long as the DJIA is above the stock's MA line, the outlook for the stock is bullish. There's room for a move up to the market average.

■ As long as the DJIA is below the MA, the outlook is bearish.

■ When the most recent additions force the stock index down through the MA, it's a sell signal. The trend of the stock is unfavorable.

■ When the most recent entries push the stock line up through the MA, it's a buy signal. The trend is favorable.

Caveats

For long-term trends, MAs can be accurate; but as shown by ITT, short-time MAs may not be very revealing. In swift market declines, especially from market tops, the signal will lag; you may lose a bundle because prices tend to fall twice as fast as they rose.

TABLE 10.1 Comparison of DJIA and ITT

Day	DJIA	ITT
1	986.87	34
2	976.65	33½
3	968.25	33¼
4	976.15	33⅞
5	972.16	33¾
6	967.25	33⅝
7	962.43	33⅜
8	968.67	33¾
9	959.03	33¾
10	962.43	34
11	963.60	34⅜

SOURCE: New York Stock Exchange as reported in *The New York Times* and *The Wall Street Journal*, February 1977.

In a congested pattern of accumulation or distribution, the MAs have a tendency to run horizontally through the center of the chart pattern; therefore it's hard to know what's happening.

To Avoid Whipsaws from False Signals

- Look for a penetration of 3% to 5% and set a specific time period, up to seven days, for the price to stay above or below the MA to be sure of the trend change.

- Or, continue the average a couple of days; i.e., with a 10-day MA, plot through the 13th day.

To Protect a Profitable Position Because MAs provide a constant frame of reference, they can be an effective way to protect a winning position, to avoid selling too soon and to boost long-term gains.

To do this, construct an MA over a meaningful time span, say 13 weeks. On the chart, plot the point marking the lowest price reached, whether this came last week, six weeks ago or at the beginning. For extra protection in erratic markets, use the closing price, not an intraday figure.

As the winning stock continues up with the usual hesitations and corrections, hold as long as the price does not break down through that low. If the stock should round over and reverse, it would quickly catch the protective MA line and get you out before serious trouble. You would also avoid being whipsawed out of a good position because of small technical reactions and the temptation to sell out too early.

This technique works just as well with short positions. In this case, the key point would be the highest price at which the stock sold in the previous 13 weeks.

- The stock price advances too fast above the MA line. Look for a technical reaction back toward the MA.

To Project It is possible to use MAs for projections by extending the trendlines. This works well with gradual changes, but it's difficult to plot MAs when the changes are short and sharp, even though there has been no major change in the overall technical action.

To offset these small aberrations, especially in bullish markets, hold the first two or three price entries. This lengthens the chart base and often creates a more stable, more predictable pattern.

To Measure Investment Performance MAs are especially valuable when used to judge investment performance of fiduciary funds such as trusts, pension funds, etc. Point-to-point measurements, unless used for very long periods of time, can be meaningless and misleading. They depend on the starting date. Short-term measurements can look good when started at a stock market low.

MAs, when plotted over 10 years or more, take into account rallies and declines, bull and bear markets, changes in economic cycles, etc. They do not entirely level out cyclical changes, but they do tend to reduce distortions caused by over- or underevaluations during any one time frame.

Compared with the overall markets, a pension fund with substantial holdings in glamor stocks would have looked sensational in the early 1970s, but dismal in 1974–1975.

When used against a stock market standard, a succession of three-year MAs, over many years, shows how well the money manager has performed. Chart 10.1 shows an example used by Wright Investors' Service, a professional investment advisory firm, in its promotional material.

Note: The MAs are based on total investment returns: price appreciation plus dividends reinvested, as reported for three-year periods, but with the last only from January 1, 1974, through September 30, 1976.

MAs are an important component in a consensus of technical indicators. Use them as a starting point for trading and investment decisions, but always look for confirmation from other sources.

Charts of moving averages of individual stocks, industry groups and

Chart 10.1   3-YEAR MOVING AVERAGE

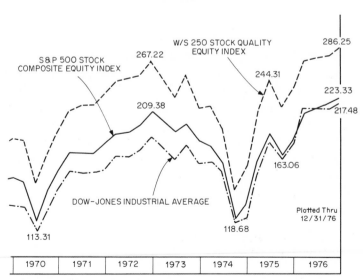

SOURCE: Wright Investors' Service.

Chart 10.2   COMPARING STOCK AND MARKET ACTION

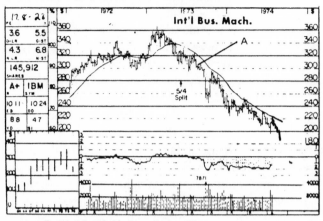

SOURCE: R. W. Mansfield, Inc., Jersey City.

standard stock market averages are available in printed forms from major services.

Compared with Stock Action

MAs can also be used to check the trend of an individual stock against its own accumulated action. In such a case, both the stock action and its MA are plotted on the same printed chart.

Chart 10.2 shows an example with International Business Machine (IBM).

When IBM was growing popular, in 1972, and at its peak in early 1973, the stock prices were, usually, above its MA. During the great fall, IBM kept below the solid line until it reached the 240 area when, for a short period, both lines converged. The stock fell again, away from the MA, signifying an unfavorable short-term future. This signal was repeated.

The basic technical rules apply: Buy when the stock line breaks out above its MA; sell when it falls below. Look for (1) a bend in the direction of the breakout, and (2) confirmation. (The first penetration, which may be false, is the warning; when confirmed, it's a signal.)

SPECIAL 200-DAY MOVING AVERAGE RATIO

An easy-to-use and accurate indicator is a special Moving Average compiled by Trendline, Inc. The chart is based on the percentage of leading

NYSE common stocks which are priced above their long-term MAs. To smooth out fluctuations, the chart is plotted on a five-week basis (see Chart 10.3).

Checkpoints

- When the percentage is above the 50% mark, the outlook is bullish.
- When the percentage is below 50%, the forecast is bearish.
- When there's a noticeable divergence from the DJIA, something is wrong: i.e., with the Dow at 1000, 90% of the stocks are above their long-term MAs. Three months later, after numerous fluctuations, the Dow is back to 1000 but only 70% of the stocks are above their MAs. Watch out.
- Internal deterioration is taking place when the DJIA holds but the percentage of MAs declines.
- An overbought-condition occurs (upward momentum fades) when over 80% of the stocks are above their MAs.
- An oversold condition occurs (the market is down to an unreasonably low level) when the chart line is down to 20% and then turns upward.

Proven Accuracy

Note how this indicator predicted market shifts:

January 1966—84% of the stocks were above the 50% line. This indicated an overbought condition and a coming bear market.

September 1966—the low of 8% was followed by an upturn, indicating an oversold condition and prospects of a future rise.

March 1969—The indicator stayed under 50%, forecasting the bearish climate which held well into 1970. The drop to 12%, in the summer, called for an intermediate rally, but since the readings did not move over 50%, the market movement proved to be a bear bounce.

May 1970—From the reading at 40%, the upmove started, signaling the start of a bull market.

Chart 10.3   200-DAY MOVING AVERAGE

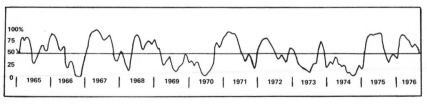

SOURCE: Trendline, Inc.

February 1971—At 96%, this was a sign of an approaching top. When the MA dropped, even though the DJIA continued to rise, it indicated trouble.

Late 1972—The DJIA was shooting up, but this indicator wasn't (it did not exceed 60%). There wasn't going to be a sustained rise.

Rules for the Sophisticated

More experienced traders, using 200-day MAs, should heed these rules, digested from recommendations developed by Joseph E. Granville:[1]

Buy signals occur when:

- The MA, following a previous decline, flattens out or advances and the price of the stock penetrates the MA on the upside.
- The price of the stock falls below the MA line while the average (base/comparison) line is still rising.
- The stock price is above the MA and declining but fails to go through and then starts to turn up.
- The stock price falls too fast under the declining MA. There's likely to be a snapback toward the MA, so the stock can be bought for a short, technical profit.

Sell signals occur when:

- The MA, following a previous rise, flattens out or is declining and the stock penetrates the MA on the downside.
- The price of the stock rises above the MA while the average line is still falling.
- The stock price is below the MA, then advances but fails to go through and starts down again.

---

[1] Joseph E. Granville, *A Strategy of Daily Stock Market Timing for Maximum Profits* (Englewood Cliffs, N.J.: Prentice-Hall, 1976).

ELEVEN

Other Indicators: Good for Signals, Better for Confirmation

There are scores of other technical indicators which, in varying forms, are used by professionals to develop more accurate forecasts. Like most technical analyses, they are subject to error, especially in interpretation. For amateurs, they are most useful as guides to trends rather than as specific signals.

With limited space, it's not possible to explain every one of these tools, but here are some of the better-known ones, including several proprietary indicators.

SHORT-TERM TRADING GUIDE

This is designed primarily for traders who move in and out of the market in days or weeks. It spotlights the intermediate-term swings which occur within major market moves.

Chart 11.1, showing the Speculative Group Activity (SGA), is based on rating the action of hundreds of stocks divided into 26 separate industry groups. Each group is classified from +2 to −2 points on the relationship of its average price for the week to a moving average (MA) of weekly prices with consideration of the direction of the MA.

The points for each group are added to form a guide value which,

Chart 11.1   INDICATOR DIGEST SHORT-TERM TRADING GUIDE

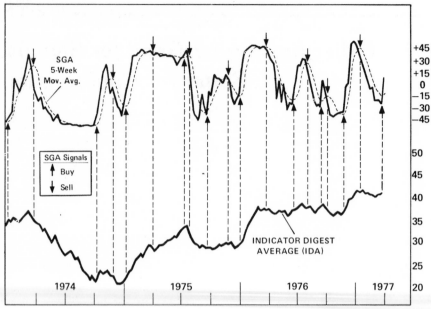

SOURCE: *Indicator Digest*, Palisades Park, N.J., 1977.

historically, has ranged from +52 to −52. These data are charted into a five-week MA.

Signals are flashed when the weekly SGA crosses the five-week MA *if* (1) both indicators are traveling in the same direction, or (2) the MA has leveled out.

Example: The SGA moves up from −54 to −42, but the MA falls from −42 to −42: No signal.

The MA remains at −43 or lower for two weeks or more, and the SGA stays above it: Buy.

On the chart, the arrows indicate action points: down, *sell*; up, *buy*.

According to *Indicator Digest*, this guide outperformed nearly all other indicators in the early 1970s.[1]

BARRON'S CONFIDENCE INDEX

This indicator is published weekly in *Barron's*. (See Chart 11.2.) It is based on the difference in yields of bonds; it is the ratio between the interest rate

---

[1]Personal conversation by C. Colburn Hardy with staff of *Indicator Digest*, Palisades Park, N.J., April 1977.

Chart 11.2   BARRON'S CONFIDENCE INDEX

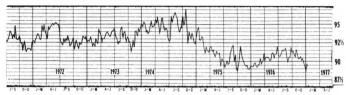

SOURCE: Trendline, Inc.

of 10 highest-grade corporate bonds and the 40 lower-quality bonds which make up the Dow Jones Bond Average.

The theory is that bond buyers are large investors who have access to excellent research and thus think, and act, three or four months ahead of the general public, as reflected in the stock market. When this "smart money" becomes more confident, the move is from high- to lower-grade bonds, so the spread narrows. And vice versa.

Thus, the Confidence Index (CI) will be high when the shrewd investors concentrate on secondary debt issues and low when they hold, and add to, top-quality bonds and thus cut their yields. As a general rule, there's confidence when the index is above 88, and doubt and/or fear when it falls to around 70.

The value of the CI is its relation to the direction of the stock market rather than to the extent of any move. For best results, watch the index over a period of time and keep comparing the trend of the changes.

Here's how the table looks:

	Last Week	*Previous Week*	*Last Year*
Barron's Best Grade bond yields	7.82	7.62	8.56
Barron's Intermediate Grade bond yields	8.56	8.53	—
Barron's Confidence Index (Ratio Best Grade to Inter. Gr. Bonds)	91.4	89.3	89.8

Since it was established in 1932, the CI has led the stock market by 60–120 days in 85% of the swings. But the length of the lead time varies, and in recent erratic years, the CI has not always caught shifts accurately. Furthermore, there is always a question as to the wisdom of "smart money."

Most CI adherents wait for minor moves to indicate similar minor moves in the stock market. The easiest way to do this is by using charts (available from *Trendline*). By drawing trendlines, it's possible to forecast the trend of the stock market.

As a general rule, studies indicate that the CI has a high degree of reliability in calling the end of a bull market but is not always so accurate in pinpointing bottoms or starts of upmoves. As in the case of most technical indicators, *Barron's* Confidence Index should be used as part of a consensus for effective forecasting of the direction of the stock market.

SIGNS OF A MARKET TOP

After you've been in the market for a while, you will catch the feel of trends. The problem is to temper your enthusiasm, or pessimism, with reliable indicators. This is where technical analysis can force discipline that will help you to sell before a top and buy after a bottom.

Here are 10 signs, summarized from *Smart Money*, to indicate that an intermediate- or long-term market top may be forming and it's time for protective action. In broad terms, the reverse means there's probably a bottom due soon.

All the data are available in the financial press. For confirmation, check the charts of major averages and leading stocks.

A top is likely when:

- The DJIA rises to new highs but the number of daily advances does not keep pace. *Rule of thumb:* For each 5-point gain in the Dow, there should be 250 more NYSE issues advancing than declining.
- The DJIA is up and the DJUA flat or down.
- The DJIA moves up with ever lower volume.
- The DJIA is up but more Most Active stocks decline than advance.
- There is heavy overall volume but little or no price gain in the averages.
- There is a very positive market: at least 400 more new NYSE highs than lows each week.
- There is a wave of public optimism: predictions of the DJIA reaching 200 or 300 points above previous peaks.
- Odd lot short sales drop to ½ of 1% of total odd lot sales.
- There is great activity in the OTC market: many low-priced stocks zooming up almost daily.
- There is a big gain in the number of call options. Speculators are using leverage for quick profits.

Don't wait until *all* of these indicators flash. A majority should be enough to start selling overvalued equities or, in a bear market, buying undervalued ones.

SPECULATION INDICES

There are several of these indicators. They relate the activity of low-priced, usually speculative stocks traded on the AMEX to securities listed on the NYSE. A major top in a bull market is marked by a sharp, almost vertical advance in such an index. When it lags behind the DJIA, the market is close to, or at, a bottom.

Speculation Index. This compares the volume of the AMEX with that of the NYSE. When the junior exchange trading is 45% or more of the Big Board, this is a warning sign. In 1968, at the height of the speculative bull market, AMEX volume rose to 60% of the NYSE, thus indicating extreme speculation and forecasting a future decline.

Barron's *Low-Priced Stock Index.* This is computed every Thursday for 20 common stocks. When this figure keeps moving up, it marks the start of a bull market. When the pace accelerates and the DJIA holds steady, beware.

Standard & Poor's Index of 20 Low-Priced Common Stocks. This is based on a portfolio, starting with $2,000, with an equal amount invested in each stock held with the 1941–1943 average equal to 10.

CD/QT (Cats and Dogs versus Quality). This is a specialty of *Indicator Digest* and has a good record of calling long-term tops and bottoms. It is the ratio of S&P's Low-Priced Common Stock Index to S&P's High-Grade Common Stock Index.

A high reading means that speculators are enthusiastic about low-priced, low-quality issues, so there's sure to be a downturn. Very low readings indicate that the speculative excesses are being wrung out and that the ground is being laid for a new bull market.

These speculation indices are most valuable at market extremes: close to tops and close to bottoms. When you are worried about such conditions, watch these technical indicators and relate them to the overall market. They are correct 90% of the time.

SPECIAL INDICATORS

Here are some useful indicators which are published in *The Financial Weekly*. Some are related to MAs, others to price and volume. All can be valuable in spotting special situations such as the beginning of a takeover or, at least, accumulation by major interests or, with downswings, loss of investor popularity.

For the most part, these are smaller corporations. But when larger companies appear for several weeks, they are usually worth checking further.

Percent of Shares Outstanding

This reports the number of shares traded in the past week as a percentage of total shares outstanding. In many cases, it's sort of a Most Active list for smaller firms.[2]

Typical Listings

Cowles Comm.	13.96
Oak Ind.	13.27
Revere Copper	8.00
Bally Mfg.	7.00
Natomas Co.	5.94

Generally, any figure above 3% indicates unusual interest; but this is relative. With smaller corporations, 5% is not uncommon. With very large firms, 2% can be significant.

Price versus Market

These tables show the 40 stocks with the highest and lowest price to market indices based on the current day's price and the price 200 days, 30 days and 5 days ago. The figures are percentages to show how much the stock has gained or lost relative to the market.

With the 30-day data, a figure of 0.5 indicates that the stock is gaining on the market at a rate of ½ of 1% per day for the 30-day period, or a total of about 15% during the time frame. During a down market, a stock could be declining but still have a plus percentage because it was declining at a slower rate than the market.

Since the same stocks tend to appear in most of these tables, it's easy to spot potential winners and follow their progress to improve trading selections and timing of transactions.

Example: Months before the takeover battle which boosted the price of stock of Milgo Electronics, the growing interest was flashed in these tables. *Do not use these tables alone. Check the charts for confirmation.*

[2]*The Financial Weekly*, Richmond, Va., Mar. 21, 1977.

Typical Listings			
High		**Low**	

Price versus market 200 days ago

Bally Mfg.	320	Johnson EF	39
Mattel, Inc.	274	Sycor, Inc.	43
Elgin Natl. Ind.	222	Heublein, Inc.	52
Menasco Mfg.	174	Purolator, Inc.	63
Harman Intl.	172	Delta Air Lines	68

Trend versus market last 30 days (%)

Mad. Sq. Gard.	+3.13	Grolier, Inc.	−2.28
Oak Ind.	+2.00	Chris-Craft	−1.36
Certain-Teed	+ .87	Mohawk Data	− .71
Sunshine Mng.	+ .78	Am. Airlines	− .61
Bally Mfg.	+ .77	Natomas Co.	− .56

Trend versus market last 5 days (%)

Basic, Inc.	+4.91	Monroe Auto	−5.41
Oak Ind.	+4.88	Scott Paper	−2.53
ASARCO, Inc.	+2.73	Fisher Foods	−2.36
Elgin Natl. Ind.	+2.56	Grolier, Inc.	−1.76
Hammermill Pap.	+2.29	Holly Sugar	−1.59

Volume: as % of 20-day moving average (calculated by dividing the week's average daily volume by the 20-day MA of volume)

Cowles Comm.	390
Vulcan Maters.	378
ASARCO, Inc.	309
Hammermill Pap.	303
Oak Ind.	229

Trend versus market last 30 days

Cowles Comm.	+18.13
Vulcan Maters.	+16.02
Oak Ind.	+ 9.96
Hammermill Pap.	+ 7.54
Fisher Foods	+ 6.58

Trend versus market last 5 days

Cowles Comm.	+99.67
U.S. Shoe	+65.45
Elgin Natl. Ind.	+57.80
FMC Corp.	+53.57
Vulcan Maters.	+50.68

COMPOSITE INDEX

This is a consensus based on information that is either available in the financial press or from your broker's technical research department. You can make your own index to get similar signals.

In this example, by Gerard Appel, the ratings run from +3 (most bullish) to −3 (most bearish). Zero is neutral. Here's how a composite looked in late 1976:

Technical indicators	Intermediate ranking	Long-term ranking
Most Active Stocks	−2	−1
Advance/Decline Lines	−1	0
30-Week Moving Average of DJIA	−2	−1
Specialist Short Sales (4-week moving average)	+2	+2
Merrill Lynch chart	−1	0
Margin Debt	+1	+1
Mutual Fund Liquidity	−3	−3
Sentiment Index	−3	−3
Cyclical Factors	+2	0
Price/Earnings Ratio	+1	+1
Short Interest Ratio	0	0
Member Short Sales	−2	−2
Dow Transportation Average	−2	0
Dow Utility Average	+3	+3
General Motors Chart	+1	+2
Dividend Yields	0	0
Width Market Trend	−2	0
New Highs/New Lows	−1	0
Interest Yields	+3	+3

The composites are: Intermediate, −6 for neutral to bullish; Long-term, +2 for neutral with a slight bullish trend.

VOLUME AND VELOCITY

To most technicians, volume is a secondary consideration. They point out that people buy and sell at a price, not at a given volume figure. They regard volume as an excellent method of confirmation of a trend:

Bullish: when volume increases with an advance

when volume decreases with a decline

Bearish: when volume increases with a decline

when volume decreases with an advance

These rules are valid but, according to Joseph E. Granville, do not take full advantage of this important technical indicator and its corollary, velocity. As he points out, "Stocks do not rise unless demand exceeds supply. Since demand is measured in volume, volume must precede price."[3] As a supplement, he also studies the velocity, that is, the rate of turnover as a percentage of corporate capitalization.[4]

Volume

A casual review of the price movement might indicate flat or unfavorable action, but deeper analysis can point up significant changes. If a stock moves up on a daily volume of 50,000 shares and then goes down on 30,000 shares, there's a net increase of 20,000 shares. This extra demand shows accumulation and, probably, the formation of a base for a strong rise.

In analyzing volume, Granville developed a special system, cumulative net volume, which he calls On-Balance Volume (OBV). Every time the stock closed at a higher price, all trading volume was added to the cumulative total. Every time the stock closed lower, that day's trading volume was subtracted from the running total. When there was no price change, no volume was recorded.

Example: Let's consider the stock of Royal Crown Cola (RCC) from October 1, 1974, to January 8, 1975. This was the period when the news about soft drinks was negative. Sugar prices were rising sharply and squeezing profit margins.

On December 18, RCC advanced by ⅛ to 6⅞. This was below the recent high, but the volume was very heavy. To Granville, this indicated that smart money was buying and such action signaled a strong upmove.

He was right. On December 19, the stock went to 7⅛. From then on, RCC moved ahead, with modest volume, to over 10 on January 6. By mid-May, the stock was at 16½.

Velocity

This is the cumulative volume as a percentage of capitalization of the corporation. It shows how many times a stock turns over and is therefore a measure of public demand. The yardstick is the OBV.

Explains Granville, "If a stock has 10,000,000 shares and records cumulative volume of 10,000,000 shares, the velocity is 100%.

"Every time the stock turns over its entire capitalization, it's like a giant spring getting tighter and tighter. When the OBV approaches 100% of capitalization, the spring will snap and the price breakout will be significant. If the stock is in a general uptrend, it will signal a sharp advance."[5]

[3]Personal letter to C. Colburn Hardy from Joseph E. Granville, Ormond Beach, Fla., April 1977.
[4]Ibid.
[5]Ibid.

Example: In late 1974 and early 1975, Occidental Petroleum (OXY) doubled in price. The volume was strong and the velocity high: 6.2% and 20.2% of capitalization, respectively. Granville's prediction: "The stock will advance far above its May 1975 level of 16⅜."[6]

By late 1976, OXY broke out at about 19 and soared to over 26 in two months. The trend was up, but the key signals came from the OBV and velocity. *Caveat:* Use these indicators only with stocks which are under accumulation, that is, moving up with ever higher net cumulative volume.

[6]Ibid.

TWELVE

Watch What the Federal Reserve Board Is Doing

Money is the lifeblood of the stock market. When money is plentiful and comparatively easy to obtain, funds flow in, the demand for stocks increases and their prices rise. When money becomes tight and interest rates rise, funds flow out of stocks into bonds; the demand for equities decreases and the value of common stocks plateau or drop.

This is an oversimplification and applies only to the intermediate- and long-term activity. But it does point out why it is always wise and, usually, profitable to watch monetary indicators catch the changes in the direction of the cost of money.

In the United States, the supply of money is controlled by the Federal Reserve Board (FRB). Its reports are not exactly technical indicators but are worth checking if only because many money managers make their decisions on the basis of their interpretations of these data. Almost always, the reports will be followed by a flurry of trading.

The most important reports are published every business Friday. They show Key Assets and Liabilities of 10 Member Banks in New York City, Member Bank Reserve Changes, Monetary and Reserve Aggregates and Key Interest Rates.

On a weekly basis, these statistics indicate fine tuning; over a longer period, at least 13 weeks, they reveal trends.

For most investors, the items to watch are the following:

Member bank reserve changes This table is important because it reports the changes in the holdings of government securities. When the FRB wants to put more money into circulation, it buys these bonds and notes from dealers (including banks), pays by check and thus makes available more funds for loans, etc. To slow down commercial lending, the Fed does the opposite: It sells securities.

Monetary and reserve aggregates This is the daily average, in billions of dollars, of the money supply. In digested form:

	One week ended	
	Mar. 30	Mar. 23
Money supply (M1), sa	314.0	315.3
Money supply (M2), sa	754.7	755.2

	Four weeks ended	
	Mar. 30	Mar. 2
Money supply (M1), sa	315.1	313.9
Money supply (M2), sa	754.6	747.9

NOTE: sa = seasonally adjusted.

M1 is the total of checking account deposits plus currency in circulation. M2 consists of currency plus all private deposits except large ones represented by negotiable certificates.

In the past week, M1 was reduced $1.3 billion and M2 was down $500 million. But over the four weeks, both rose.

Note: Always wait for confirmation, because there can be temporary swings. These take place in March, when people and corporations are preparing for income tax payments, and in December, when individuals are establishing tax losses. Both are often good times to pick up bargains.

In theory, the FRB seeks to increase the money supply at an annual rate of between 5% and 7½%. The weekly and monthly reports do not reflect velocity and other factors which are not immediately available to the public. As Fed watchers have learned, the rate of growth in the money supply must be judged over several months. Again, the important consideration is the trend. In this case, the weekly action indicates tightening but the four weeks' figures show expansion.

Key interest rates This is a weekly average of the cost of money:

	April 6	March 30
Federal funds	4.60	4.74

These rates are those of interest on loans, from one commercial bank to another, to set reserve balances. There was a slight drop here, but more important is the fact that a year ago the rate was about 5%. The flow of funds was a good omen for the stock market and, to many analysts, a positive background for an upward move.

DEFINITIVE INDICATORS

To give you an idea of how technicians use this type of information, here are three corollary indicators:

- *The discount rate:* The interest rate charged by Federal Reserve Banks on loans to banks. This was 4% in 1964, 8% in 1974 and 5¼% in early 1977.
- *The reserve requirements:* The rules governing the amount of money which member banks must maintain in FRB banks, as a percent of deposits.
- *Margin requirements:* The amount of collateral needed by investors when they borrow money from their brokers. In periods of high speculative activity, such as 1958, the Fed boosted the margin requirements to 90%. As the market moved back to normalcy and recession, the margins were reduced—to 50% in 1974, a figure which still holds. Obviously, the higher the margin, the less the borrowing, and thus the lower the demand for stocks.

These are all important signal points. When the FRB makes changes in any one, there will be shifts in the stock market. To take advantage of such situations, many technicians have developed special formulas.

Edson Gould's Three-Step-and-Stumble Rule "Whenever three successive rises occur in any one of the three rates, investors should be wary. For some time thereafter, the market is likely to suffer a substantial, perhaps serious, setback."[1]

Gould believes that the market will move in the direction opposite to a

[1]Edson Gould, *Barron's*, New York, May 6, 1968.

single change. Over 50 years, he found that his premise was correct and gave a signal 2 to 14 months prior to a market top.

Examples: When the FRB announced a third successive boost in the discount rate on December 5, 1965, the DJIA, then at 946, rose for two months to 1,011 on February 9, 1966, where it topped out. By October 10, the average was down to 736.

When the discount rate was reduced from 4½% to 4% on April 7, 1967, the DJIA, then at 853, rose to 910 by early May and to 930 by August.

Federal Indicator   This was developed by Martin E. Zweig. It measures all three factors. His approach: Add one point to a given component for each move toward easier money supply. If there's no change after six months, drop off ½ point; after two years, cancel the two points.

When all positive points are wiped out, add negative points on the next restrictive move. After one year, add ½ point; after another two years, add the remaining ½ point.

In both cases, the maximum figure is 3, plus or minus. Since these additions or subtractions apply to each of the three factors, the theoretical maximum is +9.

Actually, the swing was from +7 in 1958 at the start of the strong bull market and −5 in 1968 and 1973, both preceding bear markets.

You may not want to keep such records, but you should reassess your investment/trading strategy when there is any change in one or more of these money-controlling indicators. The Federal Reserve is signaling a change in policy. Take heed and buy, sell or sell short in anticipation of what is almost sure to happen in the near future.

THIRTEEN

How a Brokerage Firm Reports Technical Data

This is a digest of a Market Analysis Report from Merrill Lynch on January 10, 1977. This repeats items which are explained in more detail elsewhere, but it's a good example of the wide scope of readily available technical information.

DJIA 983.13	Spec. Sht. Ratio 41
P/E 10.3	ML Round Lot Short Ratio .087
5 Wk. A/D Index 55.7	Bond Stk Yield Dif. −3.45
DJ Momentum Ratio Up 7.53	

The market almost had to be disappointing in the first week of 1977, considering the substantial buying that had taken place in December and the fact that the investment services were never so one-sidedly bullish: 84.4% bulls; 9.4% bears; and 6.2% correction.

Higher than normal reserves are suggested and traders should gradually reduce exposure.

An explanation of the above terms is as follows:

DIIA: The prior day's closing of the Dow Jones Industrial Average.

P/E: The current price/earnings multiple of the DJIA—valuation measure for long-term comparisons only. Since the early 1960s, the trend has been down: in 1961 the peak was about 24; the 1966 low was about 13;

the 1968 peak around 17 to 18; the 1970 low around 11 to 12. The recent low point was 6.

5 Wk. A/D Dif Index: The five-week advance/decline diffusion index is a moving average based on the daily figures of total number of stocks advancing plus one-half of the number of stocks unchanged, divided by the total number of issues traded. One-half of the unchanged issues is added to the number of advances to give a "theoretical" percentage of the number of stocks up and to make the index fluctuate about a normal level of 0.50. It has two interpretative uses:

1. As an intermediate-term overbought-oversold indicator—

   ▪ Bull market, 57–60, intermediate overbought; 42–45, intermediate oversold.

   ▪ Bear market, 50–54, intermediate-term overbought; 36–40, intermediate-term oversold.

2. To decipher changes in the major trend when unusual readings are attained. If the major market trend has been up for some time with intermediate-term corrections of normal 42–45 readings and another correction produces a reading of 38, it would suggest that the major trend is turning down. Vice versa for an upturn. Crossings of the 50 level may be indicative of a potential trend change toward the direction of the crossing.

DJ Momentum Ratio: The average of the last 30 days' closing prices of the DJIA as part of a near-term overbought-oversold indicator, based on the difference between the DJIA close and its 30-day average. In bull markets, when the DJIA is 30 to 50 points above its 30-day average, the market is usually at its peak upside momentum and may be becoming near-term overbought and heading for consolidation. When the DJIA is 30–40 points below its 30-day average, the market is probably at peak downside momentum and may be becoming near-term oversold.

In bear markets, the near-term overbought level is 20–40 points above the 30-day average and the near-term oversold is 50–80 points below the 30-day average.

Spec. Sht. Ratio: The ratio of short sales by NYSE specialists to the total number of shares sold short on the NYSE on a weekly basis. This ratio measures the extremes of sentiment of the specialist who, in maintaining an orderly market, tends to short most heavily at market tops when nonmember buying enthusiasm is increasing. At tops, the ratio tends to exceed 60%; at bottoms, it drops below 45%.

ML Sht Ratio: The Merrill Lynch Round Lot Short Sale Ratio is the latest 5-day average of the gross Merrill Lynch short sales to total NYSE volume. Readings of 0.100 or less are a negative market indication, and readings above 0.300 are positive.

Bond Stk Yield Dif.: The bond stock yield differential which is computed by calculating the difference between the current yield on *Barron's* 10 High-Grade Bond Index and the current yield on the DJIA. Since the 1950s, bond yields have exceeded stock yields, so the figure is preceded by a minus sign. The higher the yield spread in favor of bonds, the greater the probabilities that investment money will flow from stocks toward bonds. In recent years, the market has usually made intermediate or major tops when the differential has been -4.00% or greater and has usually made important bottoms when the spread has been -3.50% or less.

Also, the Market Analysis Report regularly provides information on the technical actions of stock groups such as these:

Group Ranking S&Ls

Name	LT Trend	Med. Term	Near Term	Support-Resistance Initial	Main	
Ahmanson	N2	U3	N	14½–15	13–14	17–18
Far West Finan.	N2	U	U	8½	7½–8	11
First Charter	N2	U3	N	15–15½	14	18–19

NOTE: U = Up, D = Down, N = Neutral. 1 = In correction, 2 = Improving, 3 = Extended, 4 = Questionable, 5 = Consolidation, 6 = Losing Momentum.

Group Ranking Report

Group	Rank this week	Rank last week	Number of weeks in top 15 of last 19 weeks
REITS	1	6	3
Cement	2	15	11
Nat. Gas. Dist.	3	3	14
DJ Utilities	4	11	14

FOURTEEN

How to Find Winning Stocks

With technical analysis, you can pick winning stocks more easily, follow their progress more closely and sell more quickly, hopefully for a bigger profit and certainly for a smaller loss than you can by using only fundamental analysis.

The first step, of course, is to find stocks which are moving up and still have potential of substantial gains. When you concentrate on quality companies, you will have to search longer, accept somewhat smaller profits and have greater patience than with speculative issues. But your risks will be far less because "good" stocks are the type which attract major investors who are in a position to make substantial, continuing commitments and attract support from other professional money managers. The best stocks to buy are those which are fundamentally strong, can be expected to report even higher earnings and are becoming popular, as shown by the uptrends in price and volume on their charts.

Selection of real winners can be difficult and time-consuming; however, properly executed selections will, at best, assure relatively quick gains and, at worst, make possible quick, small losses. With quality issues, you can always count on a ready market. If you watch the charts closely and exercise strict discipline, you can achieve gains of 25% or more and keep your losses to 15% or less.

This chapter explains how to use technical analysis to find winning stocks. If you are not willing to spend the time and effort to follow these steps, get a broker who will do your homework for you.

By shifting responsibility to someone else, you will miss a lot of fun and excitement, seldom be in a position to take full advantage of technical indicators and probably have to settle for smaller profits and greater losses. A skilled registered representative can be helpful, but it's your money and it should be your decision as to what and when to buy and sell. At the outset, you may find that picking winners by technical analysis takes a lot of time, effort and research. But as you become more experienced, you should be able to spot profit makers in an hour a week.

Looking for Winners:

To find winning stocks, take these steps (not necessarily in this order):

1. *Review the weekly charts* to find formations that are beginning to point up.

2. *Check the weekly stock market tables* to discover stocks which gained two or three points or, percentagewise, outperformed the overall market by a substantial margin. In a bear market, of course, look for candidates for short sales, that is, stocks which have gone down the most.

3. *Watch the daily and weekly highs* to find popular stocks and groups. You want winners.

4. *Pay special attention to Most Active stocks.* These are the stocks in which major investors are interested.

5. *Study the Group Stock Averages* in *Barron's* and in newspapers as compiled by Associated Press. These show the percentage change, up or down, in major industries.

6. *Select 10 of the best-performing stocks* for a watch list. If there are two in the same industry, this is encouraging. Each week, add another five stocks and delete those which are no longer promising.

7. *Narrow your list to a handful of well-known companies,* preferably all traded on the NYSE, and check their quality by ratings which can be found in S&P's Stock Guide and by standards of financial strength, profitability and investor acceptance. Generally, select only those B+(Median) or higher. Avoid all weak, volatile, temporarily popular issues unless you want to speculate.

8. *Review the fundamentals* to be sure the corporations are reporting ever higher earnings and, by historical standards, are currently undervalued.

One convenient yardstick to use is the price/earnings (P/E) ratio. Some best choices are stocks which are selling below their historical range.

9. *Study three or four other leading stocks* in the same industry. You want to be sure your selections are part of a favorable trend.

10. *Look at the overall stock market.* Only rarely will any stock or any group move significantly opposite to other equities.

11. *Plot the trendline on the weekly chart* and project it as far as possible. This will mark the anticipated target price.

12. *Look at the intermediate action* for the past 12–18 months. Pay special attention to support and resistance levels. These mark points when the supply/demand equilibrium may change. Previous buyers who have sustained losses, from higher prices, will start to unload when they can break even.

13. *Get out the long-term chart* to see patterns, which usually will be repeated. Look for interim and long-term highs.

Chart 14.1 PICKING A WINNER

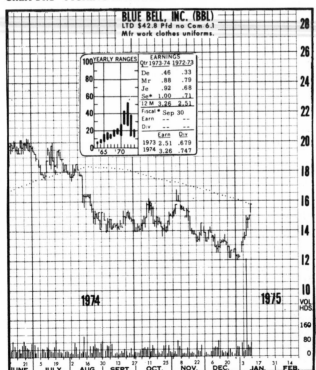

SOURCE: Trendline, Inc.

Chart 14.2   PICKING A WINNER

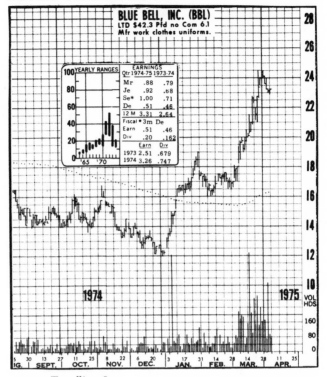

SOURCE: Trendline, Inc.

Charts 14.1 and 14.2 show Blue Bell, Inc. (BBL) in early 1975. This is a quality corporation: modest debt; high profitability (an average return of 14.4% on stockholders' equity in recent years); strong growth (almost 10% a year); and rising earnings (on a per share basis, from 67¢ in 1965 to $1.32 in 1973). The stock sold as high as 52¾ (before 2-for-1 split) in 1972 but had been hard hit by a combination of flat profits, the unpopularity of apparel stocks and the decline of the overall market.

Chart 14.1 shows an upmove from 12 to 13½—not much, but in those dismal days, promising. The last 12 months' earnings were a whopping $3.26 per share versus $2.51 for the year before. That means a price/earnings (P/E) ratio of 4.1. (This figure, rounded out, is listed in the stock market tables in the fourth column, just after the dividend.)

From your broker or advisory service, obtain the following information: (1) The historical P/E range: 15–8.2 for the 1964–1973 period. Thus, by fundamental standards, the stock is a bargain at half its lowest historical multiple.

(2) The estimated per share profits: for the current fiscal year, $3.27; for 1975, $5.00. (This information can be obtained from S&P's Estimated Earnings which lists profit projections made by leading brokers and analysts.)

From these data, make projections. At the same 4.1 times earnings, BBL would sell at 20½; at a more realistic multiple of 8, it could be priced as high as 40. So far, so good.

Now check the group chart: Textiles-Apparel. This is favorable, so review some of the other leading firms, such as Burlington Mills and Hanes Corp. Both are adding points almost daily.

Finally, study the overall market. The trend is up, from a dismal 578 to a current 635, and still rising. *Conclusion:* The market is up, the group is up and the stock is starting up. But none of these are strong.

If you are optimistic, you buy with a target of 17, that 25% gain. If you are hesitant, you wait and watch.

The next week, the stock is on the Most Active list when it jumps to 15¾. The next week it edges up, with lower volume, and then levels off in the 16–17 range.

Now the market is perking up, and mindful of the accuracy of the January forecaster, you hold (or buy) and draw in new trend lines. You have a winner, so you can project the lines and see prospects of doubling your money.

In early March there's another upmove to over 18 with heavy trading. The institutions are moving in, so you can use margin to boost your holdings. Now your trading target is 23.

From now on, most people would hold, redraw trendlines as the advance continues and, probably, set a new target at 30. Traders would move in and out, selling on strong upmoves—possibly around 23, certainly at 26—or if they missed this, on the reversal back to 23. They would buy back at 22 and set 30 as their target.

The stock continued to perform well. In September 1975, on the announcement of a 2-for-1 split, it was over 44. Then came the almost inevitable fallback to the 21 range—the 50% rule.

CHECK THE HISTORICAL PATTERN

To find possible negatives, study both the short- and long-term charts. There was an interim high at around 38, the base point for the 1973 decline. Some investors would sell to break even. This happened. The dip was small and short.

The most important point was around 52 (26 adjusted), the old all-time high. There was a decline here, but with an improving market, BBL recovered and, after several tries, broke through to a record peak of 62¾. (See Chart 14.3.)

The long-term chart (Chart 14.4) also showed the character of the stock; fairly steep V formations, up and down. When there were moves, they were quick with a steep angle. Watch for that to be repeated.

At all times, keep your major attention on that trendline. If it is clearly penetrated (10% or so), sell. When the new uptrend is confirmed, go back in. Of course, investors would be more flexible, especially when they already had a welcome profit. If the market turned down, they might sell when the stock fell back to the new trendline.

Warning: Not all stocks with uptrends perform so well or so quickly. Some do not fulfill their promise and therefore should be sold for a quick profit or loss. Others take time, sometimes as long as six months in down or erratic markets. Still others, especially those with a large number of

Chart 14.3   BLUEBELL PAYS OFF

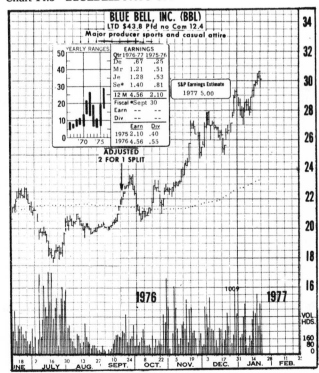

SOURCE: Trendline, Inc.

outstanding shares, will move up for a while, back off and then slowly rise again. The charts always report what is happening, not what should take place. *Obey their signals.*

Try this research/study/selection approach with charts of stocks you own and see how this form of technical analysis might have improved your selections and your timing. In one seven-stock portfolio dating back several years, following these "rules" would have meant extra profits averaging 5½ points per share: 2½ points by buying sooner and 3 points by delaying selling until the chart showed a clear reversal.

On the average, say experienced technicians, two out of every three stocks bought at confirmed uptrends pay off. Most of the losses occur when the overall market is flat or declining.

RELATIVE STRENGTH APPROACH

Another way to spot big winners early is by Relative Strength (RS). Chart services give this indicator special titles to attract subscribers, but it's still

Chart 14.4   CHECK THE HISTORICAL PATTERN

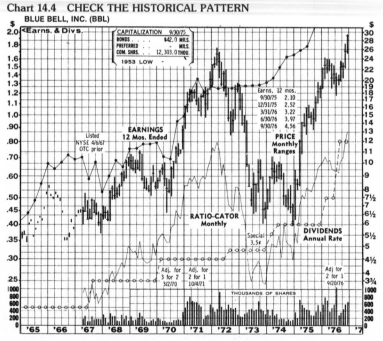

SOURCE: Securities Research Company, Inc.

Chart 14.5   RELATIVE STRENGTH

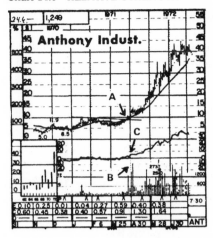

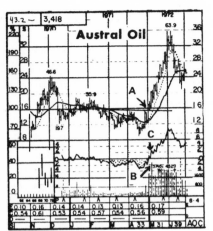

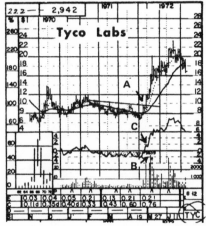

SOURCE: The Professional Tape Reader. Charts by R. W. Mansfield, Inc.

just a comparison of the action and volume of a particular stock and the overall market.

To catch the stock when it is gathering momentum for its "dazzling" upmove, look for the following:

1. *Sizable gains before the breakout.* You want to Buy High and Sell Higher. As a rule of thumb, stocks which have moved up at least 40% *before* the breakout will perform the best *after* the start of the big move.

2. *Clear indication of outperforming the market*—as shown by the RS line holding well above the indicator of the average.

3. *Heavy volume on the upside breakout.*

Three examples of the above, cited by The Professional Tape Reader, are shown in Chart 14.5.

These are the symbols: Moving Average line (A), the solid line that moves close to the stock pattern; Relative Strength Line (C), the solid line which moves around the zero mark; Volume (B), as shown by the vertical lines at the bottom.

All of these stocks had already moved up briskly: Anthony, +80%; Austral, +78%; and Tyco, +43%.

Note the very heavy volume (B) on the breakout as the prices move across the MA (A) and above the zero point on the RS line (C).

The alert trader would buy Anthony Industries at about 10, after the confirmation by A at C with super volume (B). He or she would have sold at the breakdown around 40, a 300% gain in about one year.

This approach works best with volatile, low-priced stocks which are better speculations than investments. But keep these concepts in mind when studying quality stocks too. When any issue outperforms the market, it's worth watching.

FIFTEEN

How to Use Technical Analysis to Time Selling

Smart selling is essential to stock market profits, but very few people, professionals or amateurs, are successful sellers. They either sell too soon, before full gains have been obtained, or too late, after the stock has declined and has sustained a substantial loss. If you miss a good buy, there is always another stock. If you miss a sell, you can lose money.

To do well in the stock market, you must learn how to use technical indicators to time your selling. You won't always get out at the high when the stock is moving up, and you will often take a quick loss when a stock drops, but your gains will be substantial and your losses small when you obey sell signals.

Too many people forget that the only time you can reap worthwhile returns is when a stock is moving up. You cannot increase your capital when the price level moves sideways or fluctuates within a narrow range. And you always lose money when you fail to sell at the first confirmed sign of a downturn.

With fundamental analysis, there is no way to know when to sell. You can set target prices based on past ratios, but these may be far below the ultimate value and therefore your gains will be limited. Or you can refuse to sell a stock because the long-term prospects of the company are excellent. But if the price of the stock drops 20%, what difference does your analysis make?

You can hold on and hope that, eventually, other investors will recognize the bargain price and start buying. But as most people know from experience, this can take months or even years.

Joseph E. Granville believes that fundamental analysis is "an incredible waste of time and effort as far as correctly timing the purchase or sale of any particular security."[1] He backs his view with voluminous statistics that, he believes, shows that "If earnings were important, price/earnings ratios would tend to remain the same when earnings rose: a stock, at 20, when profits were $2.00 a share, would go to 40 if earnings went to $4.00."[2]

"But," he points out, "this seldom happens." In fact, according to one detailed study, prices have a tendency to fall as earnings rise. And vice versa.[3]

Whether or not you agree with technician Granville, you must recognize that while basic values may prove out in the long run, the fundamentalist, in the meantime, is either losing money or failing to achieve capital gains while the smart technician will be making half a dozen profitable deals. As a trader, the technician may take a few fast, small losses, but he or she is also likely to pick up several substantial gains.

SUCCESSFUL SELLING

In his excellent book, *Follow the Leaders*, Richard Blackman sets 10 rules for selling which, he says, work 80% of the time. He *always* sells when any *one* of these situations occur:[4]

1. **There's a violation of the channel or uptrendline or a stock market average: DJIA or S&P's 500.** If the market flashes a down signal, get out and keep your money in a savings account until there's a clear uptrend. Here are random proofs of the value of this tough rule:

   ▪ *November 1974:* The DJIA dipped below 960 and then plummeted to 570.

---

[1] Joseph E. Granville, Ormond Beach, Fla., in letter to C. Colburn Hardy, April 3, 1977.
[2] Ibid.
[3] Ibid.
[4] Richard Blackman, *Follow the Leaders* (New York: Simon & Schuster, 1978), and personal interview by C. Colburn Hardy, February 1977.

- *July 1975:* The DJIA broke 870 and fell to 780.
- *September 1976:* The Dow broke 1000 on the way down and kept falling to almost 919.
- *January 1976:* The DJIA turned down below 980, bounced around 950 and finally dropped to below 930.

To see for yourself how to use this sell signal, plot the trendlines on the DJIA chart and find the key points.

2. **A stock reaches the top of a channel and then retreats.** Study the chart of Tandy Corp. in its upmoves during 1966–1968 (Chapter 5). Each time the stock hit the top of the channel, it retreated: in early 1967 from 3½ (adjusted) to almost 2½; in early 1968 from 8½ to 5½; etc. Plot your own channels for the other years.

When there's a new uptrend, it's OK to buy back again. A conservative might have held on through the dips and, over the years, might have scored substantial gains. But the trader would have done far better, even after commissions. "Obey the chart signals no matter what your broker tells you. In 80% of new highs, the downturn from the peak is forecast by the technical pattern."

3. **A stock's volume reaches a six-month high.** Because of the new tax law which extends the holding period for long-term capital gains, this should probably be revised to 12 months. The point is that when a stock chalks up very heavy trading, its price is at or close to a peak. When this occurs within a relatively short time after previous strong volume, it's a sell signal.

With Tandy, this was certain in early 1976, when the volume reached a super 2 million shares.

This rule provides the opportunity to sell into strength even though it might be possible to get an extra point or two by waiting for a further upmove.

"Take your profit and get out before the decline."

4. **When there are no stocks to buy.** This is the time when the market is moving sideways or down. By selling, you may miss small extra profits, but you will avoid many more losses.

"If there are no up stocks, you cannot make money. Be realistic. Liquidate and wait until things improve."

5. **After three straight losses.** If you get clobbered thrice, even when you have been playing by the rules, you should recognize that you're in a bad market. "Go into cash until you are reoriented and the market starts to move up again."

6. **After 12 months if you are fully invested.** The original rule set six months

as the time needed to qualify for a long-term capital gain, which is taxed at a lower rate than ordinary income. Under the new law, it's 12 months.

This is the time when investors with profits will start to sell a stock and depress its market. By getting out at the beginning of this dumping, you will keep your gains and avoid possible losses.

In judging the 12 months, start with the date of the first confirmed upmove of the stock, not the day of your acquisition. This will be clear on the chart. "Use this rule flexibly and with common sense. It is one of the few rules that works almost every time."

This strategy can be used with the market as a whole. Time and again, the DJIA turned down six months after the bottom from which the rise started. In the old days, when six months was the favored holding period, see how this worked:

- In the fall of 1970 from the low of early spring
- In June 1975, up from the December 1974 low

7. **When you do not understand what's happening in the stock market or with your holdings.** This is so logical that you would think that almost everyone would follow this advice, partially anyway. "Every trader should be wholly in cash two or three times a year. This gives you an opportunity to clear your head, review your objectives and look for worthwhile opportunities. If you are not making money, sell out and wait until the market is bullish."

8. **You become smug and cocky.** "Anytime you begin to think you're a genius, you're in trouble. The stock market is a tough arena where every investor competes with some of the smartest and most ruthless people in the world. Don't try to outsmart the experts. Take your profits and run."

9. **You stop making money.** You bought stocks to make money—not to break even and not to earn the equivalent of bank interest. If you can make 8% in bonds, why risk your capital unless you can gain 15% or more?

10. **There's a technical signal on the overall market.** This is always a good time to sell out or sell short. The indicators have flashed "Trouble Ahead," so why fight the inevitable? The one out of five times the charts are wrong is a small penalty to pay for avoiding unnecessary losses.

These Blackman rules are hard for most people to accept. Investors prefer to keep their money in stocks and hope for the best. They are reluctant to trade even when they realize that, when properly handled, this can assure profits. They talk of "investing for the long-term." But as has been noted, this can be a long, long time and, usually, can be very costly.

If the objective of owning stocks is to make money make more money, these rules make sense. Few people have the discipline to abide by such strictures, but those who do are likely to end up with better returns and greater capital than those who only stand and wait—and hope.

BE WILLING TO TAKE A SMALL, QUICK LOSS

No one likes to sell at a loss, but often it's the wisest tactic. It is easy to convince yourself that a losing stock will bounce back in a couple of weeks (or months), but it is seldom sensible. To technicians, such euphoria ignores the fact that one of the key criteria for stock market success is to keep your capital intact. If you lose 25% of the value of your holdings, you have to gain 33⅓% to get even.

By heeding technical indicators, you can keep your losses small and be less tempted to take unwarranted risks. Too many people who play the stock market rely on luck and refuse to recognize the odds. It's like playing poker. The chances of drawing to an inside straight are so small that the skilled card player takes such a chance only when way ahead and in the midst of a winning streak. Most of the time a card player is smart enough to fold and lose the ante money. Remember that example when the price of your stock starts to decline!

There are no 100% sure rules to help you decide whether to hold or sell a declining stock. Just how far you should let it drop depends on the size of your investment, your temperament, your financial resources, your objectives and, most of all, the action of the stock itself.

Here are guidelines. They should be used flexibly.

Limit your losses to a maximum of 15% If a stock has gone way down by 15% from your purchase price, sell. You should be concerned primarily with the preservation of the remaining 85% of your capital.

This limit applies to all actively traded shares, including those of investment companies.

Set the limit lower when you are trading on margin. This should preferably be 5% but no more than 10%. You are working with borrowed capital, and generally, will lose twice as much as you would if you were using only your own money.

In an erratic market, do not always wait for confirmed chart signals. If you buy at 30, set mental stop orders at 28½–27½ when you're trading on margin and at 25½ when you are buying outright. Most of the time, you'll be glad you settled for such a small loss.

Always sell when the uptrendline is broken on the downside. This is repeated because it is the single most important rule for successful selling.

From fundamental analysis, you may be convinced that the stock will come back, but if you want to be a good seller, get out when the downbreak is confirmed.

Once the decline starts, the odds are that the fall will continue (a trend in motion, etc.). There is no sure way to determine at what point a declining stock will stop. Today's low is often tomorrow's high.

Example: Avon Products anytime in 1973–1974. The chart tells the story. The trend was down, down, down. Shrewd traders could have made quick profits by selling short, buying back in mid-1974, selling short again, etc. But any investor who refused to sell whenever the uptrendline was broken in 1973 should have had his or her head examined!

Other Warning-to-Sell Signals:

Rampant bullishness. This occurs when everyone is making money in the stock market and nobody thinks of selling. Remember 1969 and 1970? And 1973 and 1974?

New highs in the DJIA but a lack of confirmation from the Advance/Decline line. This shows that, while the Dow stocks may be still going up, the rest of the market isn't paying much attention.

Declining volume on rallies and increasing volume on declines. The market is running out of steam; investors are becoming cautious, reluctant to buy and anxious to sell.

Three increases in the discount rate, as set by the Federal Reserve Board, in less than six months. When these raises total more than two percentage points, credit is tightened critically. That's always a bad sign for the future of stock prices.

The 200-day moving average of leading stocks, such as AT&T, IBM and GM, flattens out and the most recent averages penetrate the chart line with increasing volume. When new additions to this key indicator fail to push up the MA line, the stock market is getting ready for a reaction.

More declining stocks than advancing ones on the Most Active list. When these include institutional favorites, it's an almost sure sign of bearishness.

SUMMARY

If you are still skeptical of the value of technical analysis to time selling, review the long-term charts of stocks in your portfolio. At each downswing, ask yourself if you would have profited by heeding the sell signals. Over a three-year period, one modest portfolio would have been worth $13,000 more than it actually was!

In a broad sense, these selling rules point up the difference between technical and fundamental analysis. You may not want to obey them as fully as does Trader Blackman, but they are worth your full attention. A quick, small loss is a great deal better than a large, drawn-out one.

SIXTEEN

How to Make Money in Bear Markets by Selling Short

When you understand technical analysis, there is no reason you should not make just as much money in a bear market as you do in a bull market. You can use the same indicators in reverse. You look for unfavorable patterns that project the trends of a *down* market, *down* groups and *down* stocks. The sell short signal comes when there's a break down through the trendline. It becomes more significant when that move is through a former resistance level or below a previous bottom. Charts are even more valuable in short selling than in long buying because they report the facts without prejudice or emotion—both of which can become overly influential in depressive periods.

Despite the "tut-tuts" of so-called stock market experts, short selling is a logical, necessary and profitable technique. It takes advantage of the one sure thing about securities: Their prices will fluctuate, up and *down*. In a bull market, you buy stocks because you think their prices will advance. Why, then, is it not just as sensible to sell short when you anticipate that prices will decline?

Forget about the commissions, the idea that you are unpatriotic or have lost faith in American business or that your losses can be unlimited. Not one of these shibboleths is true. You can cut your losses by buying the stock at any point you want, and the only two reasons to invest in securities is to preserve your capital and to make as much money as you can with the least risks. In a bear market, selling short is one of the few ways you can achieve both of these goals.

TECHNIQUE OF SHORT SELLING

When you sell short, you sell stock (which you do not own) at a high price and hope to repurchase it at a lower figure. Your profit is the difference. Thus, if you sell 100 shares of Xerox short at 70 and buy 100 shares at 50, you have a gross of $2,000. You sell *high* and buy *low!*

There are special requirements for short selling:

■ The broker must borrow an equivalent number of shares, usually from other clients without cost but, occasionally, from another broker for a small fee. That permission is granted in the margin agreement you sign.

■ All short sales are on margin, which is used as collateral until the short sale is covered and the stock replaced. The margin rules are the same as for buying long: A minimum of $2,000 in cash or securities and total collateral equal to 50% of the value of the shorted stock.

■ There are no margin requirements if you own securities convertible into the stock sold short, either debentures or preferred stock.

■ Dividends received during the short position must be paid to the stock owner. That's why it's wise to short stocks with small or no dividends.

■ Short sales can be made only on (*a*) the *uptick:* when the price of the stock is at least one-eighth of a point above that of the preceding transaction; or (*b*) the *zero-plus tick:* at the same price as the preceding transaction, if that was higher than the preceding sale.

Suggestion: When there are few upticks, you may have difficulty in getting your short sale executed because other orders will have priority. To get prompt action, short less than 100 shares. Odd lots must be filled on the next round lot uptick.

USING TECHNICAL INDICATORS

When you sell short, you want an unfavorable, downtrending situation. The gloomier the market action and the more depressing the pontifications of analysts, the better the prospects for a profitable short sale.

Once in a while, an individual stock will start to decline in a flat market. This indicates that there is an unfavorable development within the group or corporation. Just as insiders start buying early when they know something good about the company, so will they start selling when they become convinced the corporate outlook is bleak.

Generally, you can find stocks to short through the same indicators as are used to pick upmovers: Most Active stocks, Highs and Lows, etc. But there's one significant difference: Only a handful of institutional investors sell short. In some cases, such a practice is banned by the charter or prospectus, but usually it's because of ignorance and/or unwillingness to face reality. This situation removes powerful forces from the market.

Before you make your first short sale, be sure you are mentally ready. With a rising stock, it's easy to let your profits run, because you already have a gain and won't be upset by temporary fluctuations.

Selling short is a psychologically difficult process. It is based on pessimism, which is hard for most people to accept, and it involves a loss when the stock does what it is normally expected to do—*go up*. Furthermore, a short seller must be willing to accept a temporary paper loss from a reaction, wait 3 to 12 months for a worthwhile profit and obey charts implicitly. It is possible to project future stock gains by fundamental analysis and, to some degree, by charts, but such techniques seldom work with price declines. Most price drops are as irrationally pessimistic as overvaluations are illogically optimistic.

FINDING STOCKS TO SELL SHORT

Some people believe that the best stocks to short are weak issues which have little support. Successful short sellers disagree. They insist that short selling should be done with shares of quality corporations when the stocks are overvalued and becoming unpopular. This is the time when professional money managers want to unload and, if fear is great enough, will accept almost any price. Such stocks will fall farther and faster than those of lower quality and value.

To find stocks which are most likely to decline:

1. *Check the chart of the overall market.* If the DJIA is trending down and shows no sign of a reversal, timing is propitious. You will be using market momentum to attain profits.

2. *Study the group stock averages.* You can find these in *Barron's*, the Associated Press weekly report and in chart services. Look for industries whose stocks are falling faster than the Dow, have dipped for at least two consecutive weeks and are the subject of pessimistic news and reports.

3. *Study the charts of the leading stocks* in these downtrending groups and pick those where the declines are confirmed and trendlines can be drawn.

4. *Review the historical chart patterns.* By doing this you can get an idea of the probable future course. If there's been a V formation on the way up, it's likely to be repeated on the decline. Look at Polaroid in 1970 (Chart 16.1), when the stock fell from about 140 to the low 50s. Then there was a rally to about 118, another dip and a rally to a new high. The formations were sharp and contained relatively few flat areas.

When the downturn came in 1973, the trend was downhill almost all the way. The same general patterns were repeated on a reverse basis.

Chart 16.1 CHARTS AID SHORT SELLING

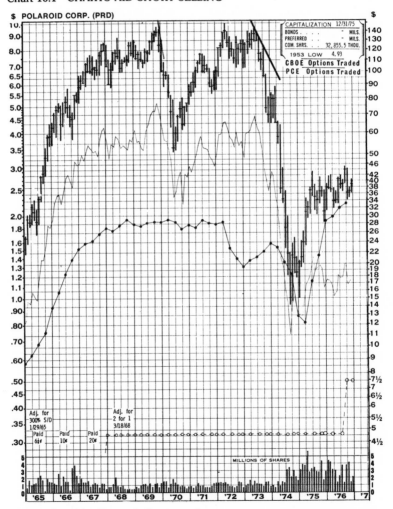

SOURCE: Securities Research Company, Inc.

For most people, the best strategy would have been to sell short in late 1973 at around 100, when the downtrend was confirmed, and buy back at around 75 for a 25% profit. When the chart continued to show a decline, you could have started selling short again in the low 60s, considered buying back at around 45 (that 25% profit) or, if you were aggressive, hold awhile.

This decision looks easy now, but at the time, the pattern was not so definitive. By the time the stock had fallen to the 30s (from a high of 149), most people were nervous and happy to get out with their gains.

They would be right, because a V formation can end quickly. The reversal can take place in less than a week and the stock can move up sharply, cutting the short sale profits. If you have hung on this long, it's wise to wait until the chart signals an upturn. You are ahead of the game and won't be hurt badly if you have to pay a few dollars more to cover your position. Such patience does take nerve, especially when you are dealing with a quality stock which you feel is already undervalued.

Experienced traders would take advantage of the interim shifts (shown best on the short-term chart) to score quick gains. Once the chart showed a confirmed downtrend, they would use the channel as a guide: selling short when the stock started down from the upper line, covering at the bottom, selling short after the 2- or 3-point bounce back, etc. Such fast moves should be made only when you do not have to pay commissions or are able to deal in large blocks.

But if you were wrong and the stock goes up to 70 by July, you will make $2,100 on the calls ($3,000 less $900 cost) to almost offset the $2,400 loss on the short sale. *Note:* The loss would be somewhat greater because of commissions.

RULES FOR SUCESSFUL SHORT SELLING

1. *Make sure that you can borrow the stock before placing an order to sell short.* It's easy, and expensive, to get caught.

2. *Sell short only when the market is headed down and projections indicate a probable decline of at least 75 points in the DJIA.* At the recent level of 950, that's an 8% dip. Without such a background, you'll have a tough time finding any stock that will drop 3 times as far to give you a fair profit.

Exception: During long, flat markets when groups of stocks are topping out or individual issues are deteriorating, you may find a few short sale candidates. Besides, this is a time when you're probably bored and looking for something to do. Be careful and limit your short sale commitments.

3. *Never sell short in a strong bull market.* Why buck the trend? In the early stages, there will be temporary sell-offs, but unless you are watchful, you can be whipsawed.

4. *Avoid volatile stocks and those with a limited number of outstanding shares.* Covering can be costly because a few small-buy orders can cause a rise rather than accelerate the decline.

5. *Short strong stocks, shares of large companies with substantial institutional ownership.* You can count on an active market as many sales will be in blocks of 10,000 or more. And when such stocks become unpopular because of overevaluation or prejudice, their prices will plummet. Only rarely will there be technical rallies to delay the ultimate decline.

6. *Target your profits 20% to 25% below the sale price.* Buy back at this level unless the overall trend is very unfavorable and the stock shows no sign of an upmove. You can always sell short again if the decline continues.

7. *Set a cover-loss price at 8% to 10% above the short sale figure.* If you're wrong, admit it early and take a small, fast loss.

8. *Watch for top patterns when the chart shows considerable resistance and there's a loss of momentum with heavy volume.* This is the time to sell into strength on a temporary rally. Very few stocks ever go straight down. Use these interim fluctuations to your advantage.

9. *Be patient.* Worthwhile drops take time and usually occur in the late stages of an overall decline. In the 1973–1974 debacle, Avon and Disney, two top glamor stocks, dropped more or less in line with the Dow at the outset but hung in for several months while the overall market kept falling. The full drop for Disney, from over 100 to below 15, took two years.

10. *Trust the charts, not your own judgment.* Never sell short just because you think a stock is overvalued. Wait until the market has confirmed this pessimism. The stock and the market do not care what you think!

11. *Be cautious on transactions toward the end of a calendar quarter.* This is the time when institutions beautify their portfolios:

- By selling, at any price, stocks which they do not want to show in their holdings. There are no requirements for investment companies and trust funds to state when the stock was sold—on March 30 or January 2. If the stock is near your target low, you may be able to get a couple of extra points by waiting a day or two.

- By buying shrewdly to boost the value of a stock just before the reporting day. What happens is this: At 3:30 P.M., the money manager gives orders to five different brokers to buy 200 shares each at ever higher prices. By the close, the stock is up sharply and the 102,000 shares in the fund portfolio are worth a lot more.

12. *Avoid stocks with substantial short interest, that is, more than 1/2 of 1% of shares outstanding.* These are issues where small traders can be squeezed if they have to cover in a hurry or, more likely, will be shot down in the cross fire of computers. This occurs when professional money managers program their computers to issue buy signals automatically when the price of a stock reaches a certain level. Just as this senseless system can trigger panic selling minutes after bad news, so the same system can boost the stock price and damage, if not destroy, a short position.

Using Calls for Protection

The most exasperating moments of short selling occur just after you have made your commitment. Often you discover that you sold too soon. A rally pushes the stock up. To protect yourself against this unnerving situation, buy options at a striking price just below your short sale figure. The profit on the options will offset the losses on the stock.

Example: In January you short 300 shares of Sears Roebuck at 62 with a target price of 50. At the same time, you buy three July calls at 3 for $900. If the stock drops, as you anticipate, your short sale profit will be reduced by the cost of the calls to $2,700 instead of $3,600.

SEVENTEEN

How to Use Stop Orders Successfully

One of the few useful aphorisms of Wall Street is "Cut your losses and let your profits run." This is easier said than done. With fundamental analysis, the long-term prospects of a company may appear so promising that you hang on with hope even though the price of the stock plummets. Or you sell when the target price is reached and thus lose out on a good chunk of extra profits.

With technical analysis, you get signals to sell quickly if the hoped-for trend reverses or to hold as long as there are profits to be made. But there is still the question of how to protect gains when you have a winner.

One effective technique is the *stop order*. This is an instruction to your broker to act when the price of the stock reaches a predetermined price. The stop order becomes a market order.

Broadly speaking, there are two types of stop orders. A *stop loss* is designed to trigger a sale when the stock hits a specific price. This protects profits or minimizes losses. The *stop limit (buy)* instructs your broker to execute an order at a limit price to which the stock moves.

Some technicians set stops, usually mental but occasionally actual, at a price 8% to 15% below their cost. They avoid round numbers and place the stop just above or below the round number, for example, 41⅞ or 42¼.

When they have a winner, traders keep moving that stop price up to retain their profits. This is called a *trailing stop order*. Carefully handled, it enables you to keep your gains as the stock price rockets. You won't get the top price, but you will end up with a sizable profit.

One typical approach in setting trailing stops is to use these criteria:

- *The last correction price*. Even in a strong upmove, stocks tend to fluctuate, moving up 5 to 6 points or dipping 2 or 3 points. Usually, the old reaction bottom becomes the new support level.

Set the stop just below that last low. If this is broken, there's not much chance of a substantial gain anyway. Take your profit and be glad you did.

- *The trendline*. When this is not too steep and is clear and well-defined, it's still the single best guide. If this is pierced on the downside, wait for confirmation but be ready to sell. Your early hopes are not likely to be fulfilled.

- *The moving average*. This preferably should be one covering a long period, such as 30 weeks. This shows the support area and should not be broken during the rise.

When two of these checkpoints come close together, you can be more confident. A stop just below such a confirmed area will probably hold. But if two of these base points are violated, get ready to sell. If three are broken, get out. There's trouble ahead.

Now let's see how this trailing stop worked with Skyline Corp. in the early 1970s (see Chart 17.1). The breakout came at 21 with the first strong move above the top of the down channel. This was a clear reversal of the earlier trend.

Set the stop at 18 (A). This will limit your loss if the stock fails to perform

Chart 17.1   SETTING STOPS

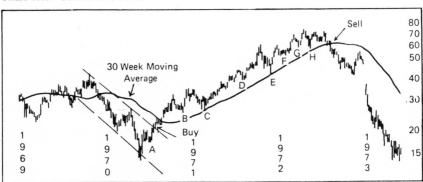

SOURCE: The Professional Tape Reader. Chart by O'Neil Datagraphs.

as anticipated. This is the correction low, approximately 10% below the cost price.

As the stock moves up to the high 30s, set a new stop at 28 (B), the next low correction price. This would mean a 15% "loss," but you're working against a profit so don't worry.

As the stock continues to rise, set new stops on the same basis: at the successive correction lows, C, D, E, F and G. Even though E looks comparatively low, it's a comfortable point because the top is under both the support/correction level and the MA.

At 60 (H), things get a bit hairy. You are almost stopped out, and the MA is getting ready to move above the stock price. But there is no confirmation of a downtrend; therefore, hold on, but make a mental note to sell just below this point, at 59⅞ or 59¾, if there's a downside break. This price is below the top, but what are a couple of points when you've almost tripled your money?

OTHER CRITICAL POINTS

Since chart patterns tend to repeat themselves, it's also wise to check past charts, especially those of intermediate-term action. This is especially helpful with volatile stocks which bounce up and down. These swinging stocks are bought by traders who are willing to take quick profits; therefore, ask yourself these questions:

What is the point at which the stock might do something it is not supposed to do?

What are the previous rally peaks?

If the stock does break down through one of these recent highs, it might keep roaring ahead. But if it fails to do this, there will almost certainly be a decline. Those traders who can now break even will start selling and probably push down the stock price.

Stops for Short Sales

Answers to these questions can be useful in short selling with erratic stocks such as National Semiconductor Corp. (NSM) (see Chart 17.2).

In June 1976, you think NSM is overpriced; and when the downtrend is confirmed, you sell short at 44 (A) The stock wiggles a bit and then heads almost straight down to the mid-30s.

But as the chart shows, this is such a swinger that it might bounce back, so you set a stop-buy order at 41⅞, just about the low point reached on two occasions earlier in the year.

Chart 17.2   STOPS FOR SHORT SALES

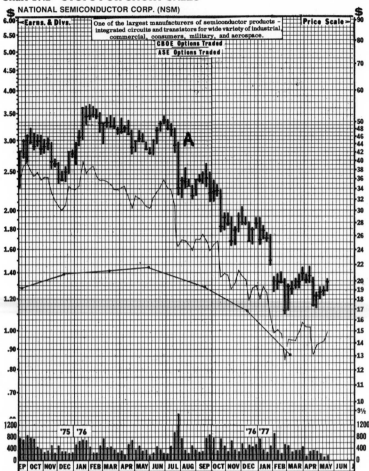

SOURCE: Securities Research Company, Inc.

The stock falls to 32, so you change the stop to 35, the low point reached eight months before. You are mindful that speculators who bought at 35 last November and took their profits may decide this is a price level at which to start buying again. If this proves true, you will still have a pleasant 9-point profit on the short sale. That's what the stop order is all about.

Whether you hold or sell and rebuy in the 28–27 area, you set the new stop at 31¾, just above the fall 1975 low. From then on, there are no useful guidelines. The stock is still declining, despite temporary rallies, so keep the short position and hope for the worst.

The best signal comes with the big gap at 22. After that disaster (for investors who own the stock), only a very determined pessimist would fail to cover the short position, especially with such a hefty profit.

Caveats for Stop Orders

Stop-loss orders are better in theory than in practice when you are trading.

In a down market a stock will slide past your price, and you can end up with a larger loss than anticipated.

Example: You buy a stock at 40 and set a stop at 35⅞. But the price slips to 38, jiggles for a few days and then—*pow!*—down to 34½ almost overnight. Since the specialist (who handles transactions in the stock on the floor of the exchange) must accept the best first price, now close to 34, your stop didn't work.

Very few amateurs enforce stops. Most people feel that stop-loss orders reflect a defeatist attitude, and being inevitable optimists, they keep lowering their selling points. How many times have you done this yourself?

Amateurs can get caught by professional trading tactics, often based on recognition of stop orders.

Example: A stock is selling at 43–44 when a big operator decides to buy 20,000 shares. It's been moving up, so this person guesses that there are plenty of stop orders at around 40. He or she starts buying, in small lots, at ever lower bids. Soon the stock is heading down.

The whammy comes when the price reaches the stop levels. Now the buyer can get all the stock he or she needs at 3 to 4 points below the first bid. By the time the purchase is completed, other investors see the bargain price and move in. Soon the price is back up to 43 and the amateurs, who relied on stop orders, wonder what hit them.

These are some of the reasons why professionals do not turn stop-loss orders over to their brokers. They make their own decisions and avoid such foolish losses.

STOP-LIMIT ORDERS

This is a technique used by professionals. When a stock is moving up toward a new or interim high, they enter an order at a price just above that high, say 71½ when the old peak was 71. If that price is reached, the stop-limit order becomes a market order and they're in business, without having to watch the tape or the next morning's paper.

These limit orders are best suited to strong stocks which are moving up into a favorable range. For most investors, they provide more pleasure than profit. Usually, the difference between the stop-buy price and the next day's quotation is seldom more than a point or so.

Stop orders of all types are valuable, but they are not substitutes for careful, frequent technical analysis.

EIGHTEEN

Technical Analysis and Options: Useful but Not Essential

One area of investing where technical analysis is supplementary is in trading options. The prices of these calls and puts are so closely related to the stock that the stock charts can be used effectively. But with the usual promotional skill of Wall Street, there are special technical services which provide charts of options, combinations of stock charts and option price projections, tabulations of percentage returns of premiums at various striking prices, probable option values at changing stock prices and so on. Few of these can be considered technical indicators, but they do provide information in handy form.

A securities option is a right to buy or sell a specified number of shares (usually 100) of a specified stock at a specified price (the striking price) before a specified date (the expiration date).

The two most important options are calls and puts: a *call* is the right to *buy* the underlying stock; a *put* is the right to *sell* the stock.

Calls on some 100 NYSE-listed common stocks and one AMEX stock (Snytex) are currently traded on five exchanges: Chicago Board of Options Exchange (CBOE); the American Stock Exchange (AMEX); the Midwest Stock Exchange; the Pacific Exchange; and the Philadelphia Exchange. In mid-1977 a limited number of puts were added.

Options listed on these exchanges have expiration dates every three months: January, April, July and October; February, May, August and November; and June, September, December and March. Prices are quoted for only three of the four maturities: i.e., January, April, July, etc. The expiration date is the Saturday after the third Friday of each expiration month.

The cost of the option is called a *premium*. Its value varies with the duration of the contract, the type of stock, corporate prospects and the general market. Premiums run as high as 12% of the value of a volatile stock with an expiration date seven months hence. With a stable stock, premiums may run as low as 3% for an option to expire in less than a month. For convenience, let's concentrate on calls.

When you write a *covered* call, you own the stock and sell the option, exercisable at a future date, for a paid-immediately sum. For example, in March you buy 100 shares of Avon (AVP) at 45 and write an October call, at the striking price of 45. For this you receive a premium of 4½ ($450). If the price of AVP stays the same or declines, the option will not be exercised. You keep the premium and the stock and can start writing new calls after October. If the price of the stock goes above 45, the buyer will probably exercise the option and you must sell the stock at 45.

Speculators often write *naked* calls (without owning the stock). They are "betting" that the price will not go above the strike price when the calls might be exercised. It's a risky business.

Call writers might use technical analysis to determine the price trend of the stock. They have a "profit" the moment they sell the call and therefore are concerned with the probable future action for two reasons:

1. To guess if the price will move *up* fast enough to trigger an early sale. This will mean a higher percentage return and an opportunity to reinvest the proceeds if the call is exercised prior to maturity.

2. To guess if the price will move *down* so much that the value of the option will decrease to the point where it becomes profitable to buy it back. For example, with Avon, if the stock fell to 40, the value of the October 45 call might drop to ½ ($50). Buying back the option at this price would cut the gross profit to $400, but now it's possible to wait until the stock rebounds and then write a new call, for January expiration, at 45.

BUYING OPTIONS

Buyers of calls look for low cost and leverage. For relatively small sums of $500 to $1,000, they can control up to 300 shares of a stock with a market value of over $10,000. Since the prices of the options and the stocks tend to move together, the $1,000 used to buy three calls of Kresge at 35 might be more profitable than the $10,500 spent to buy 300 shares outright. If the stock moves up quickly to 40, the calls will be worth at least 6 ($1,800)—an 80% gross profit. The stock profit of $1,500 will be only a 14.3% return on capital, not much for the risk.

SPECIAL OPTIONS CHARTS

Charts of stocks and options are helpful to call writers who have a profit and to call buyers who are seeking quick gains.

Chart 18.1 is typical of many proprietary services. It depicts the situation for Asarco, Inc. (AR) in early March 1977. The Trend Quality (TQ) is a 10-day moving average of quality. The TQ "tells whether a stock is acting well or whether there are subtle signs of weakness in the trading action.[1]

While the line at the top of the chart is above the base, demand is likely to be greater than supply and thus a bullish indicator. Readings below the base mean the opposite.

The Block Activity Values (BAV) at the bottom are a 10-day moving average based on the flow of transactions of 1,000 shares and larger. The BAV "tells whether big money buying or selling pressures are prevailing: above the line, predominance of demand; below, greater supply."[2] In this illustration, the demand is strong.

The Probable Options Value (on the right) are computerized estimates of the sale price of the option at any given price for the underlying stock. They are targeted five weeks ahead. Before then, the options price would probably be higher; farther away, they are likely to be lower.

This chart should be used in connection with the statistical projections. This also shows whether the stock is overbought (likely to go down) or oversold (likely to go up). Both of these figures are based on the trend of the market action.

The chart shows that the stock, at 18⅞, is in a buying range, that big money is moving in and that the option offers a profit potential. The computerized projections (in tenths) indicate the possibility of a price rise, for the stock, to 21.8 within five weeks and to 22.8 in ten weeks.

At these projections, the percentage of change will be 161.9% and 206.9%, respectively. The July 20 option, costing 1 ($100), could move to 2.6 for a $160 gross profit by early April and to 3 by mid-May for a $200

---

[1]Worden & Worden, Fort Lauderdale, Fla., Mar. 3, 1977, as confirmed by conversation with staff member by C. Colburn Hardy, Mar. 8, 1977.
[2]Ibid.

Chart 18.1 OPTIONS CHARTS

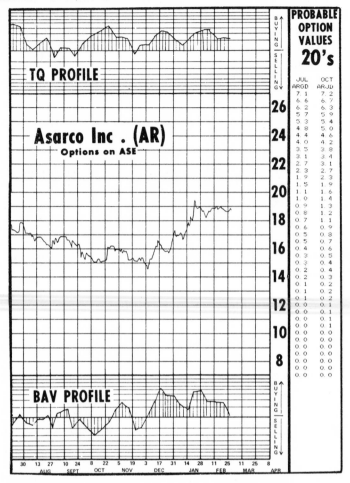

OVER BOUGHT OR SOLD	OPTION	(CODE) WEEKS TO EXP	CURR PRICE	PRICE PROJ 5 WEEKS	% CHG 5 WEEKS	PRICE PROJ 10 WEEKS	% CHG 10 WEEKS
ASARCO INC	(44)		18. 7	21. 8	+16. 4%	22. 5	+20. 5%
(-5%)	APR 15	6	3. 7	6. 8	+82. 1%		
(-5%)	JUL 15	20	4. 1	6. 8	+65. 5%	7. 5	+84. 1%
(+8%)	OCT 15	33	4. 5	6. 9	+54. 1%	7. 5	+68. 7%
	APR 20	6	0. 3	1. 8	+387. 9%		
	JUL 20	20	1. 0	2. 6	+161. 9%	3. 0	+206. 9%
	OCT 20	33	1. 3	2. 9	+113. 0%	3. 4	+148. 7%

SOURCE: Worden & Worden, Inc.

TABLE 18.1 Sample Report of Daily Percentage Returns

Contract[a] S&P[b]/exchange[c] rating	Strike price	Entry prices[d] Stock/ option	Option contract[e] Volume/ open int.	Hi/Lo prices[f] Stock/ option	Downside breakeven[g] Price/ percent	ROI[h] Time period with common at entry price strike price	Annual
AHC EG May	35	33.000	138	36/16	32.74	2.38	11.20
B+ / PB		1.250	4346	1/1	0.79	6.89	35.03
AHC HG Aug	35	33.000	36	36/16	31.91	5.05	11.01
B+ / PB		1.938	2195	2/2	3.32	9.65	21.59
AHC KG Nov	35	33.000	10	36/16	31.20	7.40	10.41
B+ / PB		2.500	73	3/2	5.47	12.08	17.15

[a]*Contract*: The name of the corporation and the symbol used by the registered representative to get the latest quotation. Here the company is Amerada Hess. The symbols: EG for the option expiring in May; HG for the August one; KG for November.

[b]*S&P*: The quality rating as determined by Standard & Poor's: B+ = median grade.

[c]*Exchange*: Where the option is traded (Philadelphia Exchange).

[d]*Entry prices*: The closing quotation of the last trading day: for the stock, 33; for the option, 1¼.

[e]*Option contract*: At the top, the number of calls, each for 100 shares of the stock, traded on the previous day: 138; at the bottom, the total outstanding contracts: 4,346.

[f]*Hi/Lo prices*: For the current year or, until June 30, for the past 12 months. These are rounded figures so provide a range rather than exact quotations.

[g]*Downside breakeven*: the price to which the stock/option could decline without a loss to the seller: 32¾ for the stock; ¾ for the call. Note that these are computer-calculated figures so, for trading purposes, should be related to the closest quotations: ⅛ point for stocks; 1/16 for options.

[h]*ROI*: Return on Investment. The next to the last column shows the percentage return for the specified time period: 2.28% for the 11-week life of the call. The last column projects this return to an annual basis. Both figures include the dividends to be received if the stock is held to expiration date and are net *after* commissions. That's why the bottom line is less. If the option is exercised, the writer will have to sell the 100 shares of stock at 35 and pay the commissions.

gross gain. The net would be cut by commissions: up to $50 for buying and selling one call, less with several options.

By referring to the figures on the side of the chart (Probable Options Values 20's), you can calculate the rewards and risks. If the stock goes to 20 at any time between March and July, you will have a small profit. If it should go to 24, you would sell, hopefully, for 4.4. If Asarco stays below 20, you have a loss.

There are many other similar services, each with special data on weeks to expiration, price projections, percentage change in the past weeks; buy signals and prices at which they will be flashed; sell signal prices; stop-loss points; and so on.

COMPUTERIZED PREMIUM
RETURNS

Some brokerage firms provide their registered representatives with daily reports of the percentage returns available from writing calls at various exercise prices and expiration dates. See Table 18.1 for an example from Reynolds Securities, Inc., an international organization, as of March 1977. *Advice:* If you become involved with options, do not enter any order until you have checked the chart of the underlying stock.

If you are writing calls, pick a stock which has just signaled a reversal from down to up. If the premium is substantial (over 10% for six months or less), write the call at a striking price close to your cost.

If the premium is small, wait until the upmove is confirmed and then try to write the call out-of-the-money (at a striking price higher than the current value of the stock).

Example: Buy Polaroid at 36 and write the call, seven months hence, at 40 for 3. Your total return will be $700 ($300 premium plus the 4-point rise), a gross return of over 19%. If the stock does not get to 40 by the expiration date, you can write a new call at 40 or even 45, depending on the strength of the overall market.

If you buy calls, do so only when the technical pattern of the stock is favorable. You make a profit only if the stock moves up briskly before the expiration date.

With long-term calls, where you expect a substantial rise, always review the intermediate- and long-term charts to see if there may be a resistance level such as a previous high, for example, at 39 with Polaroid (Chart 16.1).

If the chart indicates that your profit potential is limited, make sure that the call is priced low enough to give you a reasonable chance for a gain of at least 20%.

NINETEEN

Technical Analysis with Commodities Futures Trading

Commodities trading is different from investing in stocks, but technical analysis can be even more valuable when you are shooting for quick profits and want to keep your losses low.

When you buy a common stock, you own part of a corporation and share in its profits, if any. If you pick a profitable company, the price of its stock will move up—eventually. If you were wrong, you can sell the stock at a loss and still have capital for new investments.

With commodities, there is no equity. You buy only hope. Once the futures contract has expired, there's no tomorrow. If your trade turns out badly, you may lose all the money put up as margin.

Commodities trading involves contracts for future deliveries of raw and processed materials: food products such as wheat, corn, pork bellies, cocoa, orange juice and coffee; metals such as copper, gold, mercury and silver. There's high leverage—cash requirements of 5% to 10%. For a 40,000-pound contract on live cattle involving some $16,000, the margin is $900; for a 5,000-bushel soybean contract worth about $35,000, the margin is $3,000.

Daily price changes, limited by federal regulations, are comparatively small: 1.5¢ per pound for live cattle, 20¢ per bushel for soybeans and 10¢ per bushel for corn. But the shifts can come quickly and wipe out a trader's margin in a day or two.

IMPORTANCE OF A SPECULATOR

The economic reason for a futures market is hedging—removing or reducing the risk of a commitment by taking an offsetting position.

▪ A farmer who plants a 10,000-bushel soybean crop may sell two futures contracts at 5,000 bushels each, which call for a fixed price per bushel at harvest time. If the price of soybeans is down at the expiration of the contract, the farmer will buy back the futures for less than he or she paid. The opposite happens when the price of soybeans rises: the farmer sells the contracts for a profit. Either way, the farmer is assured of a predetermined return per bushel.

▪ A food processor who sells goods throughout the year wants a firm cost for his or her soybean purchases. This individual buys futures in the appropriate forward month. If the price rises, the processor loses money in the cash market but profits when the futures contract is sold. Vice versa when the price declines.

In both cases, the opposite side of the transaction is taken by a speculator. The speculator assumes the risk, thinking the contract can be bought or sold at a profit before the delivery date. When the speculator buys long, he or she holds the contract as long as prices rise—up to the delivery date. When selling a contract, the speculator hangs on as long as prices decline. In almost every situation, action is taken before the contract expires.

In commodities, traders lose more often than they win. The trick is to keep those losses small and to let the profits run. One big hit will more than offset half a dozen losses. Timing is very important, and that's why technical analysis can be such a valuable tool.

In using technical indicators, the basic criteria are the same: trend lines to show direction, breakouts to signal buy or sell points and patterns to use as a basis for projections of future action. But there are differences because of the nature of commodities trading:

1. All contracts are for future delivery and therefore have a limited life, usually a maximum of 18 months. Thus, projections are short and involve seasonal factors.

2. A high percentage of trading, as much as 80% in normal markets, represents commercial hedging rather than speculation. As a result, near-term support and resistance levels are not as important as with stocks.

3. The analysis of volume is much more complicated than with stocks. With securities, there are a set number of shares and every transaction indicates a change of ownership. With commodities, there is no limit to the number of contracts, and in most cases, trades are made months before anyone knows how many bushels of wheat or pounds of pork bellies

will exist at delivery time. Thus, the open interest may be far greater than the actual supply.

4. With stocks, it's possible to predict general trends of specific securities on the basis of profits, price/earnings ratios and factors more or less controllable by management. With commodities, there are unpredictable forces: droughts, floods, political price-fixing, international trade wars, etc. These can occur quickly with little warning and, often, with less logic.

5. The trendlines of stocks are better defined and thus more useful. Commodities are more volatile, and their charts seldom show the same long areas of accumulation or distribution.

There's not space here to discuss rules and strategies for the use of technical analysis with trading commodities, but here are a couple of special illustrations.

In his excellent book, *Concepts on Profits in Commodity Futures Trading* (which, unfortunately, is now out of print), Houston A. Cox, Jr., explains the Fan-Line Variation (Chart 19.1).

Using a chart of sugar: (1) Draw an ordinary trendline by connecting the high points in June and July. When this is broken, on the upside, at 2.4¢ per pound, there's a trend reversal for a couple of weeks and then a return to the original downtrend. As this continues, (2) draw another trendline . from the same 3.5¢ base. This forms the second strut of the fan.

When Fan Line 2 is broken, at around 2.2¢, there's a short upsurge and then another downtrend. When this is confirmed, draw Fan-Line 3. This is the most significant Fan Line. When it is penetrated, there's another reversal, this time one that is likely to hold.

Note that throughout this pattern, the prices tend to return toward the Fan Lines after penetration. But once the third upbreak has occurred, it's an almost sure signal of a relatively sustained period of higher prices.

The smart trader would have used this chart to:

- Sell short during the long downslide
- Cover the position on the upward penetration of Fan Line 1
- Sell short at or shortly after the intermediate peak just under 2.8¢
- Cover at the upside breakout on Fan Line 2 at 2.2¢
- Sell short, for a quick profit, before the bottom of Fan Line 2
- Move in heavily at the breakout of Fan Line 3 at the 2.2¢ area

Comments Cox, "Any hedger or speculator with futures contracts commitments tends to relax when trends are going in the direction of his position. Even though a hedger, theoretically, does not care whether the trend is up or down, costs can be less in margin when the trend is in his favor.

"And a speculator would rather count paper profits than sweat out paper

Chart 19.1   THE FAN-LINE VARIATION

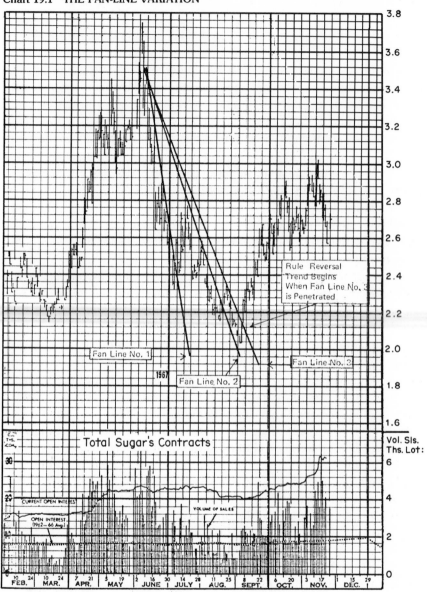

SOURCE: Houston A. Cox, Jr., *Concepts on Profits in Commodity Futures Trading* (New York: Reynolds Securities, Inc., 1972).

losses. Technical formations . . . which occur in the trend development
. . . make it easier to reassay their market programs."[1]

TECHNICAL INDICATORS AID PYRAMIDING

Technical analysis is also valuable in pyramiding, that is, using profits to
acquire more positions as the price of the commodity rises.

At the outset of each commitment, Cox sets points of "abandonment"
(when the market moves against his original judgment) and "entry" (when
he's right and wants to add to his holdings).

To keep the risk-loss factor in line, Cox tends to set the maximum initial
abandonment (stop-loss) at 50% of the per contract margin; i.e., for a
margin of $1,000 per contract, at a price where the maximum loss will be
$500. He shifts that sell point up as the price of the commodity rises.

Cox keeps his eyes on two lines: the regular trendline and the moving
average line. He buys in additional units of $1,000 when he has a basic
profit and both indicators are moving up. He limits his pyramid commitment to three units. And he always sells promptly when the trendline
breaks down through its support level.

[1]Personal conversation by C. Colburn Hardy with Houston A. Cox, New York, Smith
Barney Co., April 1977.

Chart 19.2 SAUCER FORMATION

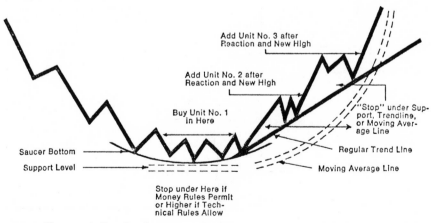

SOURCE: Houston A. Cox, Jr., *Concepts on Profits in Commodity Futures Trading* (New York:
Reynolds Securities, Inc., 1972).

His goal: a 50% profit on the capital engaged. He stays with a trend as long as possible but makes a technical check at the end of each trading day. If he has his profit, he reviews the situation, and unless the overall market is strong and the chart pattern (Chart 19.2) still above the key lines, he considers selling. With commodities, you can never afford to be careless or overly hesitant.

POINT & FIGURE CHART OF COMMODITIES

Chart 19.3 shows a variation of the standard P&F chart in that there are two figures: X's to denote a rising price; O's to indicate a falling one. These are 3-point reversal charts; three boxes of price changes are necessary before one moves from X's to O's or from O's to X's. Once a direction has been established, each 1-point change in the same direction is recorded. Both can never be in the same column. Both record the daily highs and lows, not the closing prices.

Chart 19.3 POINT & FIGURE CHART FOR COMMODITIES TRADING

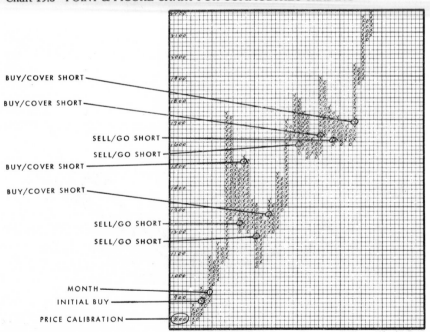

SOURCE: Chartcraft, Inc.

As with all technical indicators, watch for trends and reversals. When the trend is up, consider buying; when it turns down, it's a sell signal to get out of a long position or to move into a short position. How fast you act depends on your capital, your experience and whether you wait for confirmation which, on this type of chart, occurs quickly.

To Keep the Chart Up-to-Date

If the current column is an X one, check the daily high. If this is above the previous close, add the X in the same column and ignore the daily low. If no X's can be drawn, check the daily low to determine whether a reversal has occurred. If not, make no entries.

If the current column is an O one, check the daily low. If this permits the drawing on one or more O's, add them and ignore the daily high. If you cannot draw more O's, look at the daily high for signs of a reversal. If there's been one, move to the next column and draw the appropriate number of X's. If there's been no shift, make no entries.

There can never be X's and O's drawn on the same day. There's either a continuation of the current column or a reversal or no new entries are made.

Signals

Buy:

- When an uptrend is established. Aggressive traders often start buying after two X's have been recorded; more conservative ones usually wait for three X's.
- When a column of X's rises one box higher than the highest X of the prior X column.
- To cover a short position, at your price objective or at the same point as your buy signal. Since this can be determined in advance, you can enter a stop-loss order here.

Sell:

- When a downtrend is confirmed (at least two O's and preferably three).
- When a column of O's declines one box below the lowest O on the prior O column.
- To close out a long position, at a target price or at the same point as your sell signal. This is determinable in advance to protect your holdings.

Bullish: When a buy signal is flashed and until a sell-short signal is flashed.

Bearish: When the most recent signal is to sell short. This holds until a buy signal occurs.

Pullbacks: For less risk, rather than act immediately on a signal, wait until the reversal is confirmed by at least one more move in the direction of the new trend.

TWENTY

Technical Rules and Lore

Repetition often can be boring, but in this guide it is used to emphasize important information. This chapter is sort of a catchall. It repeats some of the most important rules of technical analysis, adds some new advice and attempts to provide a ready reference when you are wondering what to do, when you are wondering why the market has not acted as you anticipated and when you are tempted to relax discipline. As with most rules—and all technical analysis—there are exceptions, but here's wise counsel from the experts.

RULES FOR TECHNICAL ANALYSIS

1. *For investment, choose stocks which move within a narrow range. For trading, buy volatile issues which move up and down sharply.* Try to exploit extremes by buying near lows and selling near highs.

2. *In both investing and trading, look for a minimum potential move of 15%* —quickly with trading, and up to a year in investing.

3. *Maintain discipline.* Have a system and stick to it.

4. *Never trade with money you are saving for basic expenses* such as a new house, vacation, car, education, etc.

5. **Be realistic.** Never become overly optimistic or pessimistic. As long as you stick to quality stocks, you will always make money eventually. Technical analysis will make those profits come earlier and cut your losses more quickly.

6. **Be patient.** Wall Street is often slow to recognize value. When there are millions of shares of stock outstanding, it can take a long time to significantly change the supply/demand relationship.

Worthwhile gains take time: with trading, at least three months; with investments, 18–24 months.

7. **Cut your losses.** Always be ready to sell for a quick, small loss if you have made a mistake, the market turns against you or the stock fails to perform as anticipated.

A trader should sell when the chart shows a break down through a trend line of 3% to 5%; an investor should consider selling with a drop of 10% below cost; always act with a 15% loss.

8. **Let your profits run.** When the stock has moved up to your target price, set a stop (mental if you can keep watch; actual if you can't). This will lock in your gains. If the stock continues to rise, raise that sell price accordingly.

9. **Place stop orders at fractions just below or above whole numbers,** for example, 49⅞ or 50¼. A trader is more likely to give a broker an order to buy or sell at 50 or 55 than at 50⅛ or 55½. The great majority of orders on the specialist's book will be in round numbers.

10. **Do not reverse your position** unless there are new, strong factors and the chart action is confirmed by other technical indicators. If your original research was carefully done, it was probably correct. The commissions on switches can eat up your profits.

11. **Double up when you have a winner.** If the chart trend line continues up and forecasts an even higher price, add to your holdings as long as there is a good possibility that there can still be a further 15% gain. But be ready to sell when there's a downside breakthrough.

12. **Never boast about your investment/trading skill.** People who talk about their successes usually have losses to hide. What you do with your money is your own business.

13. **Never buy or sell against the overall trend of the stock market.** No matter how promising a stock looks, do not buy unless—and until—there's a favorable trend in the stock group and the market.

When any stock moves against the tide, there must be something special afoot: a merger, acquisition, new product, etc. Even with inside information, the odds are against a worthwhile move by the time the news is public.

14. ***Don't average down.*** That is, don't buy more shares of a losing stock. All you are doing is to increase the extent of your potential losses. Once a stock starts to decline, there's no way to predict its bottom price. Take your losses and put the proceeds to work in promising situations.

15. ***Act promptly.*** In trading, timing is the key. When the chart action has been confirmed, move in hard and fast: buy on the uptrend and sell on the downmove. The confirmation can come from the chart or, better, from other technical indicators.

STOCK MARKET LORE

1. *Be cautious when there's a 30-point week.* When the DJIA moves up or down 30 or more points in five successive trading days, this is usually a forecast for a correction. When this big move comes in a rising market, take your profits and wait. When it takes place in a down market, get ready to buy early the following week. The rally may be temporary, but chances are good that you can pick up bargains and make a few, quick points.

2. *Act after a 100-point move.* When the market soars 100 points, get ready to sell. A reversal is likely. Such a strong move is the ideal time to score big profits. The gains on the first 20 points will be modest, but from then on, it's all gravy. Let your profits run, but when the rise is 90 points or so, think about cashing in.

Conversely, when there is a long, sharp decline, watch that 100-point mark. You should get out of the market, with most holdings, after the first 20-point drop. Or start selling short. Hang in there on the short sale as the decline continues. But be ready to cover your position when the 90-point drop is passed. This is the time when there will be panic selling. Even this won't last forever, so take your profits and wait for the ultimate rise to be confirmed.

3. Most major bottoms occur in the last half of the year and, almost always, at intervals of 4 to 4½ years.

4. If there's a three-phase bull market cycle over about 32 months, look for a bear market lasting 16–22 months. The entire cycle seldom lasts more than 48–54 months.

5. When the number of advances outnumber the declines and the DJIA advances, the market is likely to continue up.

6. If the quality of the market leadership (more solid Blue Chips on the Most Active List) coincides with an upmove of the DJIA, the advance will probably continue.

TABLE 20.1 Characteristics of Bull and Bear Markets

	Phase 1	Phase 2	Phase 3
Bull markets			
Advance Decline line	Has stopped going down and moved above previous interim high.	A top equal to or higher than that of phase 1.	Records major peak at end of phase 2 and generally diverges from DJIA.
Highs and lows	Since previous low climax, new highs consistently outnumbered new lows.	Never as many new highs at one time in bull market as new lows in bear markets. New highs not expected to top out until late in phase 2.	The final attempt, by new highs, to scale earlier peak fails. Increase in new lows, but seldom passes new highs.
Dow Jones Industrial Average (DJIA)	Since DJIA low confirmed by DJ Transports, clear pattern of rising bottoms and tops.	Will make a new bull market high very late in phase 2, after mid-phase correction.	In its glory, pulling away from other indices. Series of new highs climaxed by sharp, perpendicular rise, not confirmed by most indicators.
50% principle	If DJIA is retraced more than 50% of previous completed bear market decline, strong evidence of Bull phase 1.	No major function.	No important application.
General Motors	In early part, drops to lowest level in 4–4½ years, usually after Dow bottom. Once refuses to make new low for 4 months, confirms bull market.	Trends higher through phase 2.	Tops out ahead of DJIA.
Secondary offerings	Very few. A period of accumulation, not distribution.	Normal amount.	Very frequent.
Stock splits	Stock prices too low.	Too early for many.	Great frequency.
Short interest	Not very dependable at this stage.	Tends to drop; fluctuates between 1.00 and 1.50.	Not a reliable indicator at market tops.
Odd lot short sales	If peaks at 15,000–50,000 in few weeks after major bottom, definitely in Bull phase 1.	Rather dormant.	Very low: 1,500–3,000 area.

Bear markets			
Advance Decline line	Breaks under low recorded just prior to bull market rally in Blue Chips.	Turns up strongly out of down channel, then breaks down sharply, usually through previous low.	Continues to zigzag to new lows.
Highs and lows	Number of new lows up and soon surpassed by new highs.	New highs for year outnumber lows, but not for long.	Almost no new highs while lows climax in the 500–900 area.
Dow Jones Industrial Average (DJIA)	Sharp declines from peaks; rally in 60 days, then break to new low and zigzags down.	One or two stocks get back to old high, but such spot strength soon gives way to primary bearish trend.	Most Dow stocks make new lows with handful responsible for most losses.
50% principle	The earlier activated, more valid likely to be. If more than 50% of previous bull market retraced earlier, probability of new bear market low.	If activated, very bearish, predicting a new low below that of previous bear market.	If activated in this phase, chances strong that DJIA close to bottom and there may be a bear trap.
General Motors	Now bearish. Downside break and generally trending down.	Tacks on only few points in mid-phase rally. Then breaks to new low.	Continues to make new lows, with almost no support for stock.
Secondary issues	Continues with great frequency.	Pass peak.	Almost none.
Stock splits	Still continue but slowing.	Very few.	Almost none.
Short interest	Sharp decline.	Starts to go up, then one more large decline on mid-phase rally.	Rising rapidly as more people sell short on bad news.
Odd lot short sales	Starting to build, up to 5,000–8,000 area.	Generally in 5,000–8,000 area.	Possible sharp rise late, probably after Dow bottom. Watch for unusual activity.

SOURCE: Joseph E. Granville, A Strategy of Daily Stock Market Timing for Maximum Profits (Englewood Cliffs, N.J.: Prentice-Hall, 1976), pp. 223–236. (Confirmed by letter to C. Colburn Hardy, Apr. 3, 1977.)

7. If the majority of most active stocks are up, the advance will continue the next day.

8. A strong closing market usually means a good opening the next day, if there has been no dampening news overnight.

9. If the price of gold moves up sharply for three days, the fourth day the market will probably be down or, at best, neutral.

10. After three sharp declines, the market will usually slow and about half the time will rebound.

11. No sustained advance is likely until the DJIA has gone up four successive days. Three-day rises are common. The *go* signal often is flashed when the upmove continues for the fourth and, better, fifth day.

12. BUY on any decline that follows a confirmed advance. You'll make a few extra dollars.

13. BUY into any unconfirmed decline. This is almost always a temporary fluctuation which will be followed by a continuation of the advance.

14. NEVER BUY into a decline that follows an unconfirmed advance. You're asking for trouble.

15. NEVER BUY into a confirmed decline. No matter what the long-term prospects of the stock may be, the market has spoken.

16. SELL on any advance that follows a confirmed decline. You should have sold earlier, but if you hesitated, get out with this advantage.

17. SELL into any unconfirmed advance. The odds are that this will be followed by the forecast decline.

18. NEVER SELL into any advance that follows an unconfirmed decline.

19. NEVER SELL into a confirmed advance unless the stock has moved past your target price. Even then, you'll do better to let your profits run.

CHARACTERISTICS OF BULL AND BEAR MARKETS

See Table 20.1 for Joseph E. Granville's characteristics of bull and bear markets, as digested from his *Strategy of Daily Stock Market Timing for Maximum Profit*.

Glossary of Investment, Stock Market and Technical Terms

(Based on definitions from publications by The New York Stock Exchange, Richard Blackman, James Dines, James L. Fraser, Joseph E. Granville, *Indicator Digest*, William L. Jiler, Harvey A. Krow, John Magee, Robert A. Mansfield, Merrill Lynch, Kenneth Ward and John Winthrop Wright)

ACCUMULATION: That which results from a stock which shows higher volume on the upside than on the downside. Generally, this is a period of price equilibrium after a decline. The forces of demand become dominant, and the trend of the stock turns up.

ADVANCE/DECLINE LINE (A/D): A line, plotted on a cumulative basis, that shows the difference between the number of stocks advancing and the number declining each day. A declining A/D marks the beginning of a downward trend but should be confirmed by other indicators before action is taken. A rising A/D line is a sign that the market is moving up.

ADVANCE/DECLINE RATIO: The number of stocks advancing divided by the number of stocks declining over a set period, such as a day, a week or a month.

AVERAGES: Various methods of measuring the trend of the stock market or a security.

AVERAGING DOWN: Buying additional shares of a stock as it declines in price. A foolish policy that usually expands losses.

AVERAGING UP: Buying additional shares as the price of the stock rises. A good technique with a winner.

BAR CHART: A chart which shows price, time and volume. For each time period, usually daily or weekly, the high and low price of the stock is recorded as a vertical line with a nub to denote the closing value. Time intervals are shown on the horizontal axis. Volume is indicated by vertical bars at the bottom of the chart under the applicable price data.

BEAR: Someone who believes the market will decline.

BEAR MARKET: A declining market. Bear markets are always shorter in duration than the bull markets preceding them. Major bottoms are seldom more than 4½ years apart.

BEAR TRAP: Any technically unconfirmed downmove that encourages investors/speculators to be bearish. It usually precedes strong rallies and often catches the unwary.

BIG BOARD: Popular name for the New York Stock Exchange.

BLOCK: A single transaction of 10,000 shares or more.

BOTTOM: The low point of a stock or market, clear only through hindsight. This is the point where most people are convinced the worst is yet to come. It's the best spot to buy for maximum gains.

BREADTH: The net number of stocks advancing versus those declining. When advances exceed declines, the breadth of the market is declining. When the reverse happens, it's negative.

BREAKOUT: What occurs when a stock price or average moves above a previous high resistance level or below a previous low support level. The odds are that the trend will continue.

BROKER: An agent who handles the public's orders to buy or sell securities, commodities or other property. Also known as Registered Representative or Customer's Man.

BULL: One who believes the market will rise.

BULL MARKET: Any rising stock market, usually with three definable phases and a duration longer than that of the preceding bear market.

BULL TRAP: Any technically unconfirmed move to the upside that encourages investors/speculators to be bullish. Usually precedes important declines and often fools those who do not wait for confirmation by other indicators.

CALL: An option to buy a specified number of shares of a stock, usually 100, at a specified price before a specified future expiration date. Calls on over 100 NYSE-listed stocks are traded on special options exchanges.

CAPITAL GAIN OR CAPITAL LOSS: The profit or loss from the sale of capital assets such as securities. Under current federal law, a capital gain is short-term when attained in less than 12 months; long-term when the property is held over one year. A short-term gain is taxed at the individual's full income tax rate. A long-term gain is subject to a lower levy of one-half of the full tax rate, generally to a maximum of 25%. All capital losses are deductible, to varying degrees, on income tax returns.

CAPITALIZATION: The total amount of securities issued by a corporation (bonds, debentures, preferred stock, common stock) plus surplus.

CD/QT (CATS AND DOGS VERSUS QUALITY): An *Indicator Digest* average based on the ratio of S&P's Low-Priced Common Stock Index to S&P's High-Grade Common Stock Index. At the start of a bull market, this index is usually around 1.00. With optimism, the ratio rises to as high as 3.00 in periods of unusual speculative fever. Conversely, it falls sharply during corrections.

CHANNEL: The trading range for a stock as shown on a chart. It is the space between the two parallel lines marking the extremities of the configuration recording the price movement of a stock or average. The slope represents the direction of the trend. Traders buy when the price of the stock is at or near the bottom of the channel and sell when it's near or at the top.

CHART BREAK: When the price of a stock breaks through a previously unviolated level: bullish on the upside; bearish on the downside.

CHARTING: The use of graphs and charts in the analysis of stocks, commodities and markets to plot trends of prices, averages and volume.

CHURNING: Unethical trading of a customer's account, by a broker, to create extra commissions.

COLLATERAL: Securities or other property pledged by a borrower to secure repayment of a loan.

COMMISSION: The cost of trading securities. This cost is lower, percentagewise, with larger orders.

COMMON STOCK: Securities which represent ownership interest in a corporation. Common stockholders assume greater risk than do owners of bonds or preferred stock, but generally they exercise greater control and may gain greater rewards in the form of dividends and capital appreciation.

CONFIDENCE INDEX: A weekly index published in *Barron's* that shows the ratio of the yield of 10 highest grade bonds to the yield of the broad Dow Jones 40-bond average. The ratio varies from the middle 80s (bearish) to the middle 90s (bullish). Its value has been questioned, but it is often useful in confirmation of trends shown by other technical indicators.

CONGESTION AREA: A relatively confined, neutral trading range where the supply and demand balance out.

CONSOLIDATION AREA: A pause in a trend, usually followed by a further move in the same direction as that of the previous trend. A bad time for making money.

CONTRARY OPINION: The belief opposite that of the general public and Wall Street.

It is most significant at major market turning points. An overall consensus of opinion, whether bullish or bearish, usually marks an extreme. An investor taking a contrary view will usually benefit in time.

CORRECTION: A reversal of a major trend. A term often used by puzzled analysts.

COVER: To offset a previously placed futures transaction—a call, short sale or commodities futures contract—with an equal and opposite transaction.

CUSTOMER'S MAN: Stockbroker.

CYCLE: An interval in which a stock or market completes a movement and returns to its original state. Cyclical stocks are those of industries whose profits move up and down in fairly well-defined patterns: steels, machine tools, construction, automobiles, etc. With the market, there are four stages: bear market, upturn, setback and bull market.

DAY TRADE: Buying or selling on the same day. This requires minimal margin but is best suited for professionals who pay no commissions.

DEFENSIVE: With stocks, tending to remain fairly stable in a declining market. With markets, selling stocks short or moving from equities into fixed income holdings when there are signs of a bear market.

DEFENSIVE INDEX: Measurement of the ebb and flow of quality, conservative capital such as contracyclical stocks. *Indicator Digest* bases its index on such equities as American Natural Resources, American Electric Power, General Foods, Pacific Telephone and Wrigley.

DISCOUNT: (1)(n.) The amount by which a preferred stock or bond may sell below its par value. (2)(n.) The amount by which shares of closed-end funds sell below their net asset value. (3)(v.) To take into account, as in "the price of the stock has discounted the expected dividend cut."

DISCOUNT RATE: The interest rate which is charged to member banks who borrow money from the Federal Reserve System.

DISCRETIONARY ACCOUNT: An arrangement whereby the owner of securities gives written power of attorney to an investment adviser or broker to make buying and selling decisions without notification to the holder. Often wise with fiduciary funds; seldom so with trading accounts.

DISPARITY: A term used to indicate the difference between the movements of the Dow Industrials and S&P's 500 Stock Index. When the Dow moves up faster, it's bearish. Conversely, when the Dow lags, it's bullish.

DISTRIBUTION: When the supply of a stock is greater than the demand, usually shown by higher volume on the downside than on the upside. It's a sign that smart investors are unloading on the public. Such action will force down the price of the stock.

DIVIDEND: The payment, authorized by the Board of Directors, to be distributed pro rata among the shares outstanding. On common stocks, it is about 50% of profits, more with utilities. Fundamentalists consider dividends an important factor in total investment returns. Technicians are not so impressed.

DIVISOR: The factor which is divided into the Dow Jones Averages to calculate the daily average. Recently, the divisors were 1.504 for the 30 industrial stocks, 2.567 for the 20 transportation stocks and 3.912 for the 15 utilities. The divisor is changed with stock splits and stock dividends.

DOUBLE BOTTOM: The result of a stock, or average, when it reaches similar levels of technical support. The advance from the second bottom is usually stronger and steeper than that from a single bottom; so, too, with declines.

DOW JONES INDUSTRIAL AVERAGE (DJIA): The standard stock market average which shows the market action of the stocks of 30 major corporations on a price-weighted basis. DuPont, at 150, has 5 times as much impact as does Woolworth at 30.

DOW JONES TRANSPORTATION AVERAGE (DJTA): A standard index based on the market action of the stocks of 20 airlines, railroads, shipping· firms and trucking companies.

DOW JONES UTILITY AVERAGE (DJUA): A standard index based on the market action of the stocks of 15 electrical utilities and gas companies.

DOWNSIDE: A technical term to indicate the possible degree of risk for a stock or market on a decline.

DOWNTICK: A security transaction which occurs at a lower price than the previous transaction.

DOWNTREND: A chart pattern that shows that the value of the stock or market is declining. Opposite of UPTREND.

DOW THEORY: A theory of market analysis based on the performance of the Dow Jones Industrial and Transportation stock prices averages. The market is in a basic uptrend if one of the averages advances above a previous important high and is accompanied or followed by a similar advance in the other. When the averages both dip below previous important lows, this is regarded as confirmation of a basic downward trend.

EXHAUSTION: When buying power is no longer enough to force an advance. Vice versa on the downside.

EXTENDED: The term used for a stock which has advanced or declined to, or is in excess of, its trend configuration. Often preliminary to consolidation.

EXTRA: A short form of "extra dividend." A payment in the form of stock or cash in addition to the regular or usual dividend the company has been paying.

FALSE BREAKOUT: An abortive movement out of a seemingly genuine continuation pattern of a stock or market. To be sure that the breakout is for real, wait for confirmation by the same or other indicators.

FEDERAL FUNDS: The money borrowed by banks which belong to the Federal

Reserve System from other member banks to meet reserve requirements when there's a deficiency.

FEDERAL FUNDS RATE: The rate of interest on interbank loans (federal funds). This reflects instantaneous pressures in the supply of and demand for bank reserves. It is a sensitive indicator of the level and direction of interest rates over the near term. A high or rising rate usually forecasts higher costs of money. A low or falling rate indicates that banks are not in as great a need for reserves and therefore lower interest rates are likely.

50% PRINCIPLE: If a previous decline in the market is more than 50% retraced on the next rally, the market is likely to retrace its full decline. Conversely, if an advance is more than 50% retraced on the next decline, the market will probably retrace the entire advance.

FISCAL YEAR: A corporation's accounting year. Some corporations do not use a calendar year for their bookkeeping: e.g., department stores, because of heavy Christmas sales, wind up their accounting on January 31. Thus, their fiscal year is from February 1 of one year through January 31 of the next.

FLAT BASE: A long period of price fluctuations in a narrow range. When accompanied by accumulation, this forms a platform for a strong breakout.

FLOATING SUPPLY: The amount of stock which is readily available, not closely held. With a small float, there can be a squeeze on the price of the stock and a decline is likely.

FUNDAMENTAL ANALYSIS: Research of industries and corporations on the basis of such factors as sales, assets, earnings, profitability, growth, products, services and management. The opposite of technical analysis.

GAPS: On charts, the visible separations in consecutive price levels, for example, from a closing price of 23 to a next day's opening at 24½. They are bullish in early stages of an up-price move, bearish in late stages of a decline.

GLAMOR AVERAGE: An *Indicator Digest* average made up of stocks considered market leaders. Their action provides clues as to which way the market is headed. It is generally considered an index of professional speculative confidence.

GROWTH STOCK: Stock of a company with a record of growth in earnings at a relatively rapid rate.

HEAD & SHOULDERS (H&S): A chart configuration that portrays three successive rallies and reactions, with the second reaching a higher point than either of the others. The failure of the third rally to equal the second peak is a warning that a major uptrend may have come to an end. Conversely, a bottom H&S, formed upside down after a declining trend, suggests that an upturn lies ahead. No H&S should be regarded as complete until the price breaks out below the neckline, drawn tangent with the lows of the Left and Right Shoulders.

HIGH-LOW DIFFERENTIAL: The difference between the number of new highs and the number of new lows. Similar to the Advance/Decline line. This exposes the underlying strength, or weakness, in the market, not always apparent with a standard average.

HOLD: A favorite term of advice from analysts who recommended buying a stock and now find that its price has dropped.

INDEX: A statistical yardstick expressed in terms of percentages of a base year or years; for example, the Federal Reserve Board's index of industrial production.

INDICATOR DIGEST AVERAGE (IDA): An unweighted average of 1,500 NYSE stocks. The original base was 50. Each day there's an addition or subtraction of a figure representing the average of the percentage changes in all NYSE stocks for that day.

IN-OUT: Purchase and sale of the same security within a short period, such as a day, a week or even a month. An in-and-out trader is generally more interested in day-to-day price fluctuations than dividends or long-term growth.

INSTITUTIONAL INVESTOR: An organization whose primary purpose is to invest its own assets or those held in trust by it for others. Includes pension funds, investment companies, insurance firms, universities and banks.

INTEREST: Payments a borrower makes to a lender for the use of money. A corporation pays interest on its bonds to bondholders; a speculator pays interest to the brokerage firm for borrowing in a margin account.

INVESTMENT: The use of money for the purpose of making more money through `income from interest or dividends or to increase capital or both. Safety of principal is an important consideration.

INVESTMENT COMPANIES: A company or trust which uses its capital to invest in other companies. There are two principal types: *open-end*, or mutual fund, which sell new shares to investors and stand ready to buy back old shares; both at the net asset value of the securities in the portfolio; *closed-end*, with a limited number of shares which are traded like stocks and whose prices reflect demand and supply.

INVESTOR: An individual whose primary concerns in the purchase of a security are regular dividend/interest income, safety of original investment and, if possible, capital appreciation.

LEADING INDICATOR: Any statistic or guide which moves ahead of the market or the economy. The stock market is a leading indicator of the economy.

LEVERAGE: (1) With an investor, the use of existing assets (cash, savings or securities) to acquire other securities. (2) With stocks, the use of margin to borrow money from a broker. This permits ownership of more securities than could be obtained with cash alone. Hopefully, there will be benefits in additional dividends and appreciation. (3) With a corporation, the effect on the per share earnings of the common stock of a company when large sums must be paid for bond interest or preferred stock dividends, or both, before the common stock is entitled to a share of the profits. Leverage can be advantageous when profits are good but may be harmful to common shareholders when earnings decline, because with highly leveraged, debt-heavy companies, a high percentage of income must be used to pay fixed charges.

LIMIT ONLY: Stated by a customer, the maximum price at which the broker can execute an order to buy or the minimum price at which the stock can be sold.

LINE FORMATION: A long, fairly flat movement shown by a chart. When this occurs, it is building a base for a breakout.

LIQUIDITY: The ability of the market in a particular security to absorb a reasonable amount of buying or selling at reasonable price changes. It is one of the most important characteristics of a good market. Usually, the more shares outstanding, the better the liquidity. Thinly capitalized stocks (under 3 million shares outstanding) are usually less liquid and more volatile than larger issues.

LISTED STOCK: The stock of a corporation which is traded on a securities exchange.

LONDON AVERAGE: The London Financial Times Index of the action of a select group of stocks traded on the London Exchange. It is sort of a British DJIA and is useful in predicting the direction of the NYSE.

LONG: Signifies ownership of securities. An investor who owns 100 shares of General Electric is "long."

M PATTERN: A chart configuration showing double top with the right leg falling below the support level in the middle of the formation. At the point where the decline is greater than before, sell short.

MARGIN: The amount paid by customers when they use their broker's credit to buy a security. Under Federal Reserve regulations, the initial margin required in the past 20 years to buy stocks has ranged from 100% to 50% of the purchase price.

MARKET ORDER: An order to buy or sell a stated number of shares of a security at the most advantageous price obtainable after the order is entered on the floor of the exchange.

MEMBER FIRM: A securities brokerage organization with at least one officer who is a member of the NYSE.

MOMENTUM: The rate of acceleration in expansion of price or volume. Upside momentum is greatest just before a top; downside momentum is greatest at or near a major bottom.

MOMENTUM INDICATORS: Market indicators, usually moving averages, related to price and volume. They are used to determine overbought or oversold conditions and the underlying strength or weakness of a market trend.

MOMENTUM RATIO: The difference between the closing price of the DJIA and the 30-day moving average of this stock market standard. When the Dow is well above its moving average, the market may be heading toward a top. When it's well below, the down momentum may be near its end.

MOVING AVERAGE (MA): A technical indicator formed by adding daily data for a set period of time, such as 10, 30, 100 or 200 days. Once the time unit is complete, the first number is dropped and the next day's data added: i.e., with a 10-day MA, day 1 would be deleted when day 11 is added. Technicians use MAs to (1) smooth out daily, short-term fluctuations; (2) compare stock or group movements with those of a standard stock market average; and (3) discover trends. When the MA stays above a rising line (of a stock or average), it's a bullish signal. Vice versa for a bearish forecast.

NEAR TERM: Generally, a period of three to five weeks.

NECKLINE: With Head & Shoulders formations, the line drawn between the low points of both shoulders. When this is broken on the downside, it usually marks the beginning of a sharp and extended decline.

NET CHANGE: The change in the price of a security from the closing price on one day and the closing price on the following trading day. The net change is the last figure on the stock price list in the financial press. The mark +¾ for General Motors means that the price of each share advanced 75¢.

NEW YORK STOCK EXCHANGE (NYSE): The major auction market for common stocks and corporate bonds, where buyers compete with other buyers and sellers compete with other sellers for the most advantageous price.

NYSE COMMON STOCK INDEX: A composite index covering price movements of all common stocks listed on the Big Board. It is based on the close of the market on December 31, 1965, and is weighted according to the number of shares listed for each issue. Point changes are converted to dollars and cents to provide a measure of price action.

ODD LOT: Stock purchased in units of less than 100 shares.

ODD LOT SHORT SALES: The amount of stock sold short in odd lots. This figure indicates the expectations of small, usually uninformed investors that the market will decline. Rising volume of this indicator signals a bull market is near because these odd lotters are almost always wrong.

ON BALANCE VOLUME: A cumulative volume figure whose direction depends on price movement. A positive change in price indicates that the volume for that particular time interval is positive and the indicator will move upward. Vice versa for a downtrend. (See Granville's theories on page 103.)

OVERBOUGHT: Term used to describe the price level at which momentum can no longer be maintained and so the stock or market has no place to go but down. This condition occurs after a sharp rise during a period of vigorous buying. It is a point at which, some technicians say, prices become too high.

OVERHEAD SUPPLY: An area where selling can be expected. This is a price range slightly higher than that of current quotations. Records of previous highs or resistance points indicate that there are likely to be more shares for sale than are now being traded.

OVERPRICED: Term used to describe a price level at which an analyst feels a stock is selling at considerably more than its true value. Some fundamentalists believe that this level is reached when a stock trades at a price/earnings ratio higher than that of the past. They would recommend selling. Technicians would hold the stock as long as its trend is favorable, because they believe that the price reflects supply and demand, not value alone.

OVERSOLD: Term used to describe a security or market that has declined to an unreasonably low level. This condition is characterized by an increasing excess of net daily declines and, frequently, forecasts a reversal and rally.

OVER-THE-COUNTER (OTC) MARKET: The trading market for shares of companies not listed on stock exchanges. A few are stocks of large banking and financial organizations, but most are of small, unseasoned corporations. In this market, dealers buy for and sell from their own inventory.

PAPER PROFIT: An unrealized gain on a security still held. Paper profits become realized profits only when the security is sold.

POINT: (1) With shares of stock, $1. If a stock rises 3 points, each share is worth $3 more. (2) With market averages, point means just that: The DJIA rises from 950.25 to 951.25 and is therefore up 1 point.

POINT & FIGURE CHART (P&F): A chart on which price activity is recorded without reference to time intervals or volume. The stock price is posted in a square one above or below another, depending on the upward or downward movement of the stock price. When the price shifts direction, the chartist moves to the next column to record the new price.

PORTFOLIO: Holding of securities by an individual or institution. May contain bonds, preferred stocks, common stocks and other types of securities or property.

PRICE ALERT: That which results when a stock exceeds its highest or lowest price at which it has traded over the last 75 days.

PRICE/EARNINGS RATIO (P/E): The price of a share of common stock divided by earnings per share for the last 12 months. A stock selling at 40, with annual profits of $4.00 a share, has a P/E ratio of 10. The price/earnings ratio is used by fundamental analysts to determine the relative value of a stock and to project its future price range. Technicians argue that, since earnings lag the market by nine months, this guide is of little immediate use. They believe that the current price of a stock has already discounted future earnings.

PRICE OBJECTIVE: Technical appraisal of the stock's future value. May be projected by continuing the up-slanting trendline.

PRIMARY TREND: The predominant movement of the stock market in any phase. When it's up, it's a bull market. When it's down, it marks the beginning of a reaction or, when continued, a bear market.

PROFIT-TAKING: Selling stock which has appreciated in value since purchase. Also, an analyst's attempt to explain a downturn in the market following a period of rising prices.

PULLBACK: The result of a stock or market when it falls back from a previous advance.

QUOTATION (QUOTE): The highest bid to buy and the lowest offer to sell a security in a given market at a given time.

RALLY: A brisk rise following a decline in the general price level of the market or an individual stock.

REFLEX REACTION: A movement in the opposite direction of a stock's trend which does not break or reverse that trend but corrects an overbought or oversold condition.

REGISTERED REPRESENTATIVE: A full-time employee of a member firm of the NYSE who has met the requirements of the NYSE as to background and knowledge of the securities business. This person handles purchases and sales for customers and receives a commission for such services.

RELATIVE STRENGTH LINE: A line on a chart which shows the price performance of a stock or group in comparison with a broad market index. To compute, divide the price of the stock by the market index for each time period and connect the resulting plotted ratios with a line.

REPORTS: Written documents prepared by security analysts for clients or brokerage firms and investment advisory services. Usually they are verbose and inconclusive and provide information which has already been acted upon by major investors.

RESISTANCE: A price level where potential sellers overcome demand and temporarily stop or reverse an advance. This is usually the point at which several advances have stopped and from which declines have occurred.

REWARD/RISK RATIO (R/R): A calculation of the possible gain versus the possible loss. If an investor believes a stock can rise from 25 to 40 or fall to 20, the R/R ratio is 15 points up, 5 points down. This is a favorable 3:1 ratio.

SCALE: To buy or sell over a period of time at increasing or decreasing prices, such as at 20, 22, 19, 23. A technique used by institutional investors to average purchases or sales.

SECONDARY OFFERING: A public sale of stock owned by a few individuals, usually officers or directors of a corporation. Such a sale seldom benefits the company.

SECURITIES AND EXCHANGE COMMISSION (SEC): The federal agency established by Congress to help protect investors. Address: 500 North Capitol, N.W., Washington, D.C. 20549.

SELL AT MARKET: To accept the best available price for a stock.

SELLING CLIMAX: Exceptionally heavy volume created when panicstricken investors dump stocks. Often this marks the end of a bear market and is a spot to buy.

SHAKE-OUT: A strong technical correction where there's a short, sharp decline.

SHORT COVERING: Buying stock to return shares, previously borrowed, to close out a short sale.

SHORT INTEREST: The total number of shares sold short. The figure for NYSE- and AMEX-listed stocks is released four business days after the 15th of the following month. This standard indicator is widely used by technical analysts. A large short interest can be bullish, because it indicates positions which must be covered by buying stock. Short interest must be related to overall volume. To adjust for this, analysts use the short interest ratio.

SHORT INTEREST RATIO: The ratio of the monthly short interest to the average daily trading volume for the reported month. When the ratio is under 1.00, the outlook is bearish. Above 1.50, it's bullish. This ratio is better to forecast bottoms than tops.

SHORT SELLING: Selling a stock not owned in anticipation of buying it back at a lower price for a profit. This is accomplished by having your broker borrow the stock from another investor. When you sell short, you incur an obligation to return the stock at some future time by buying shares back, hopefully at a lower price. When short selling becomes heavy, it may mark the beginning of a rally.

SPECIALIST: A member of the NYSE who (1) acts as a broker's broker and (2) maintains an orderly market in the stocks in which he or she is registered as a specialist. The specialist buys or sells for his or her own account, to a reasonable degree, when there's a temporary disparity between supply and demand.

SPECIALIST SHORT SALES RATIO: The number of shares of stock sold short by specialists. Professionals sell short after the market has risen substantially and seems ready to reverse its course. A normal level is around 55%. At 40%, this indicator is bullish; over 67%, it's bearish.

Since specialist short sales can constitute as much as 65% of all short sales, a high specialist short interest is very bearish.

SPECULATION: The employment of funds by a speculator.

SPECULATION INDEX: The ratio of the monthly AMEX volume to that of the NYSE. This ratio seeks to measure the level of public speculation. When the ratio moves above 44%, a caution signal is given as the market is nearing a top. When the ratio is under 31%, it marks public apathy or bearishness.

SPECULATOR: One who is willing to assume a relatively large risk in the hope of gain. This person's principal concern is to increase capital rather than to receive income from interest or dividends. The speculator may buy or sell the same day or speculate in an enterprise which he or she does not expect to be profitable for several years but still has tremendous potential.

SPLIT: The division of the outstanding shares of a corporation into a larger number of shares. A 3-for-1 split by a company with 1 million shares outstanding results in 3 million shares. Each holder of 100 shares now owns 300, but their value is one-third of the former per share price.

STABILIZATION: A period of sidewise price movements, usually visible before a trend reversal. Similar to accumulation after a decline and top formation or distribution after an advance.

STANDARD & POOR'S CORPORATION (S&P): An organization which provides statistical data about stocks and bonds, publishes a number of investment-oriented services and charts and maintains special stock market averages. Address: 345 Hudson Street, New York, N.Y. 10014.

STANDARD & POOR'S 500 STOCK INDEX: This is made up of the stock market action of 500 major corporations listed on the NYSE: 425 industrials, 20 railroads and 55 utilities. It is weighted by market value and the number of outstanding shares of the component corporations.

STOCK DIVIDEND: A dividend paid in securities rather than in cash.

STOP ORDER: An order to buy a stock at a price above or sell at a price below the current market. Generally, it is used to limit losses or to protect unrealized profits in a short sale.

SUPPORT: A barrier to a decline. The level at which the buyers continue to equal the sellers. May be a base for an upmove.

SWITCH ORDER: An order for the purchase (sale) of one stock and the sale (purchase) of another stock at a stipulated price difference.

TAPE READER: One who watches the ticker tape to determine the probable future action of the market or a stock. The tape reader believes that the ticker tape is the net sum of all the hopes, fears, greed and pessimism of everyone in a position to act in the stock market.

TARGET: The price level to which a stock appears likely to move: a sell point when the trend is up; a buy point for covering a short sale. Often this is projected by extending the trendline on a chart.

TECHNICAL ANALYSIS: The study of the market and stocks based on supply and demand. The technician watches price movements, volume and trends/patterns which are revealed by charting these factors. From these data, he or she attempts to assess the possible effects of current market action on future supply and demand and acts accordingly. The technician is concerned with what *is*, not what *should be*. The opposite of fundamental analysis.

TECHNICAL BREAKOUT: That which results when a stock or market moves through a point of previous resistance. Generally a signal of higher prices to come.

TECHNICAL CORRECTION: The correction, downward, of the price level after momentum pushes it up too far. Vice versa for a declining situation. The shift often is one-third to one-half of the rise or fall.

TECHNICAL INDICATOR: A device employing deductive logic to forecast stock prices. It involves reasoning backward rather than forward. The tools of technical analysis—trend lines, chart formations, volume, Advance/Decline lines, moving averages and other factual criteria—used to project movements of stocks, industry groups and the overall market.

TECHNICAL RALLY: A reaction from a previous trend. The movement of the market is always in swings and almost always moves down too far. The technical rally is a reaction upward after such a downswing.

TECHNICAL REACTION: What occurs when prices move in one direction for a time and then, with little or no excuse, reverse.

TECHNICIAN: One who relies on stock market action and indicators and pays secondary heed to fundamentals.

THIN MARKET: A market for a stock in which there are comparatively few bids to buy or offers to sell, or both. Price fluctuations between transactions are usually larger than when the market is liquid.

TOP: A high for a market or a stock.

TOPPING OUT: A peak point where the sellers begin to outnumber the buyers.

TRADER: One who buys and sells for his or her own account for short-term profits.

TRADING INDEX (SHORT-TERM): The ratio of the Advance/Decline ratio to the upside-downside volume ratio. Favorable when significantly less than 1.00; unfavorable when significantly more than 1.00.

TREND: The direction of a price movement. A trend in motion is assumed to remain intact until there is a clear change.

TRENDLINE: On charts, the line drawn to connect the last 2 or 3 low points of a stock's price action. This is one of the most important technical tools. It shows the support level which technicians watch carefully in order to buy when the trend is up and sell when there is a break down through the trendline.

TRIANGLE: A chart pattern where a stock fluctuates in progressively smaller price ranges, similar to winding up like a spring for a breakout. An ascending triangle foreshadows an upside breakout. A descending triangle precedes a renewed decline.

TRIPLE BOTTOM: Three support levels at similar points. If this formation occurs in the last stage of a bear market, it is a strong buy signal.

TRIPLE TOP: Three high points at about the same price level. The last top is the point from which a sharp decline is likely to occur. If this formation takes place in the third phase of a bull market, it's a sell signal.

TURNOVER RATE: The volume of shares traded in a year as a percentage of total shares listed on an exchange. For an individual stock, trading volume as a percentage of outstanding shares.

UNDERPRICED: A term used to indicate the price of a stock which some analysts feel is below its true market value. When a stock is selling at a price/earnings ratio below its average range for the past decade and corporate prospects are good, fundamental analysts consider it underpriced.

UPTICK: A transaction which occurs at a higher price than that of the previous transaction.

UPTREND: A chart configuration which shows that the stock or market is moving to higher levels, even though there may be interim fluctuations downward.

V FORMATION: A chart pattern showing a sharp decline, a quick turn and a sharp ascent, or the reverse.

VELOCITY: Total cumulative volume as a percentage of capitalization of a corporation. It is important on the buy side and often is an advance clue to either a takeover or some other dynamic corporate development.

VOLATILITY: The degree of intraday or interday fluctuations, not necessarily concerned with price movements over a period of time.

VOLUME: The number of shares traded in a security or a market during a given period, usually reported on a daily or weekly basis. On a Bar chart, it is represented by vertical lines at the bottom of the chart.

VOLUME ALERT: A signal resulting from a stock's volume exceeding its 60-day moving average of volume by some predetermined criteria.

W PATTERN: A formation on a chart that looks like the letter W. A breakout above the middle leg is bullish.

YIELD: With stocks, the dividends expressed as a percentage of the current price of the security. A stock at 50, with an annual dividend of $2.00 per share, has a yield of 4%.

YIELD DIFFERENCE BONDS/STOCKS: The spread between the interest paid on bonds and the dividend return of DJIA stocks. In recent years, the bond yields have been more than 4% greater than the return on stocks. Historically, the spread has ranged below 2%.

References ━━━━━━━━━━━━━━━━━━━━━

BOOKS

INVESTMENTS AND THE STOCK MARKET

Amling, Frederick, *Investments* (Englewood Cliffs, N.J.: Prentice-Hall, 1970).

Bowyer, John W., Jr., *Investment Analysis* (Homewood, Ill.: Irwin, 1972).

Crane, Burton, *The Sophisticated Investor* (New York: Simon & Schuster, 1964).

D'Ambrosio, Charles D., *Guide to Successful Investing* (Englewood Cliffs, N.J.: Prentice-Hall, 1969).

Dougall, Herbert E., *Investments* (Englewood Cliffs, N.J.: Prentice-Hall, 1973).

Emory, Eric S., *When to Sell Stocks* (Homewood, Ill.: Dow Jones-Irwin, 1973).

Engel, Louis, *How to Buy Stocks* (New York: Bantam, 1971).

Farrell, M. L. (ed.), *Dow Jones Investors' Handbook* (Homewood, Ill.: Dow Jones-Irwin, 1974).

Findlay, M. Chapman, and E. E. Williams, *Investment Analysis* (Englewood Cliffs, N.J.: Prentice-Hall, 1974).

Graham, Benjamin, *The Intelligent Investor* (New York: Harper & Row, 1973).

Graham, Benjamin, *Security Analysis* (New York: McGraw-Hill, 1962).

Hagin, Robert, and Chris Mader, *The New Science of Investing* (Homewood, Ill.: Dow Jones-Irwin, 1973).

Hardy, C. Colburn, *Dun & Bradstreet's Your Investments* (New York: Thomas Y. Crowell, 1978–1979 (annual).

Hazard, John W., *Success with Your Investments* (New York: Doubleday, 1973).

Jessup, Paul F., *Competing for Stock Market Profits* (New York: Wiley, 1974).

Kent, William A., *The Smart Money* (New York: Doubleday, 1972).

Lishman, John M., and David T. Crary, *The Investment Process* (Scranton, Pa.: Intext, 1970).

Loeb, Gerald M., *The Battle for Investment Survival* (New York: Simon & Schuster, 1965).

Loeb, Gerald M., *The Battle for Stock Market Profits* (New York: Simon & Schuster, 1970).

Peisner, Robert N., and Darryl Peisner, *How to Select Undervalued Stocks* (New York: Dutton, 1972).

Phelps, Thomas W., *100 to One in the Stock Market* (New York: McGraw-Hill, 1972).

Rukeyser, Louis, *How to Make Money in Wall Street* (New York: Doubleday, 1974).

Shulman, Mort, *Anyone Can Still Make a Million* (New York: Stein and Day, 1972).

Widicus, Wilbur W., and Thomas E. Stitzel, *Personal Investing* (Homewood, Ill.: Dow Jones-Irwin, 1971).

SPECIAL SECURITIES

Clasing, Henry F., Jr., *The Dow Jones-Irwin Guide to Put and Call Options* (Homewood, Ill.: Dow Jones-Irwin, 1975).

Darst, David M., *The Complete Bond Book* (New York: McGraw-Hill, 1975).

Fried, Sidney, *Investing and Speculating with Convertibles* (New York: Crown, 1975).

Gastineau, Gary L., *The Stock Options Manual* (New York: McGraw-Hill, 1975).

Noddings, Thomas, *Guide to Convertible Securities* (Homewood, Ill.: Dow Jones-Irwin, 1976).

Noddings, Thomas C., and Earl Zagore, *CBOE Call Options* (Homewood, Ill.: Dow Jones-Irwin, 1975).

Thomas, Conrad W., *Risk & Opportunity*, (Homewood, Ill.: Dow Jones-Irwin, 1974).

Wendt, F. C., *Investment Guide to Profits from Rights, Splits and Dividends* (New York: Pilot Press, 1974).

Zieg, Kermit C., and Perry J. Kaufman, *Commodity Trading Techniques* (Homewood, Ill.: Dow Jones-Irwin, 1976).

STOCK MARKET

Blackman, Richard, *Follow the Leaders* (New York: Simon & Schuster, 1977).

Cohen, A. W., *Point and Figure*, Larchmont, N.Y. 10538, Investors' Intelligence.

Dines, James, *How the Average Investor Can Use Technical Analysis for Stock Profits*, P.O. Box 22, Belvedere, Calif. 94920, 1972.

Edwards, Robert D., and John Magee, *Technical Analysis of Stock Market Trends* (Springfield, Mass.: John Magee, 1975).

Fosback, Norman G., *Stock Market Logic*, Fort Lauderdale, Fla. 33306, Institute for Econometric Research, 1976.

Gillett, Clarence H., *Stock Market Timing*, Larchmont, N.Y. 10538, Investors' Intelligence.

Gordon, William, *Stock Market Indicators as a Guide to Market Timing* (Palisades Park, N.J.: Investors' Press, 1968).

Granville, Joseph E., *New Key to Stock Profits* (Englewood Cliffs, N.J.: Prentice-Hall, 1963).

Granville, Joseph E., *A Strategy of Daily Stock Market Timing for Maximum Profits* (Englewood Cliffs, N.J.: Prentice-Hall, 1976).

Huang, Stanley S., *Techniques of Investment Analysis* (Scranton, Pa.: Intext, 1972).

Jiler, William L., *How Charts Can Help You in the Stock Market* (New York: Trendline, Inc., 345 Hudson Street, 1972).

Markle, Daniel R., *Relative Strength and Stock Market Timing* (Alton, Ill.: Trader's Research, 101 Cherry Street, 1975).

Seamans, George, *The Seven Pillars of Stock Market Success* (Brightwaters, N.Y.: Windsor Books, 1974).

Wheelan, Alexander H., *Study Helps in Point and Figure Techniques*, 150 Broadway, New York 10038.

Williams, Larry, *How to Select Stocks for Intermediate and Substantial Gains* (Brightwaters, N.Y.: Windsor Books, 1973).

MAY BE OUT OF PRINT

Barnes, Robert M., *The Dow Theory Can Make You Rich*, (New Rochelle, N.Y.: Arlington House, 1973).

Bishop, George W., Jr., *Charles H. Dow and the Dow Theory* (Englewood Cliffs, N.J.: Appleton Century Crofts, 1960).

Hamilton, William P.: *Stock Market Barometer*, La Jolla, Calif.,: Dow Theory Letters, Inc.

Krow, Harvey, *Stock Market Behavior* (New York: Random House, 1969).

Rhea, Robert, *Dow Theory* (New York: Barron's, 22 Cortlandt Street).

CHART AND TECHNICAL SERVICES

Chartcraft, Inc., One West Avenue, Larchmont, N.Y. 10538:
  NYSE & AMEX, weekly, $180.00 per year; monthly, $192.00 per year.
  OTC, quarterly, $72.00 per year.
  Weekly Review, $72.00 per year.
  Weekly Commodity Service, $180.00 per year.
  Weekly Options Service, $150.00 per year.

Commodity Research Bureau, Inc., 1 Liberty Plaza, New York, N.Y. 10006:
  Futures Market Service, $85.00 per year.
  Commodity Chart Service, $245.00 per year.
  Daily Commodity Computer Trend Analyzer, $545.00 per year.
  Special charts: Wheat Futures, $125.00 per year; Soybean Futures, $95.00 per year.

M. C. Horsey & Co., 120 South Boulevard, Salisbury, Md. 21801:
  NYSE, Bimonthly, $70.00 per year.

Harry Lankford, Box 213A, Wichita, Kans. 67201:
  NYSE, weekly, $210.00 per year.
  AMEX,, weekly, $181.00 per year.
  OTC, weekly, $174.00 per year.

R. W. Mansfield Co., 26 Journal Square, Jersey City, N.J. 07306:
  NYSE, AMEX and OTC, for one service, monthly, $125.00 per year; every other week, $230.00 per year; weekly, $435.00 per year.

Securities Research Company, 208 Newbury Street, Boston, Mass. 02116:
  3 Trend Security Charts, monthly, $59.00 per year.
  Wall Charts, quarterly, $12.00 per year.
  3 Trend Cycli-Graphs (12 years), quarterly, $37.00 per year.

Trendline, Inc., 345 Hudson Street, New York, N.Y. 10014:
  Daily Basis Stock Charts, $280.00 per year plus postage.
  Current Market Perspectives, monthly, $84.00 per year plus postage.
  OTC Chart Manual, bimonthly, $75.00 per year plus postage.

Daily Graphics, William O'Neil & Co. P.O. Box 24933, Los Angeles, Calif. 90024:
  NYSE, weekly, $499.00 per year; combined, $938.00.
  AMEX, biweekly, $495.00 per year combined, $495.00. monthly, $160.00 per year combined, $290.00.
  Stock Option Guide, weekly, $98.00 per year

TECHNICAL ADVISORY SERVICES

The Advisor, Box 13645, Houston, Tex. 77019.
Burns-Kirkpatrick Letter, 49 Riverside Avenue, Westport, Conn. 06880.
Chartcraft, Inc., One West Avenue, Larchmont, N.Y. 10538.
The Chartist, Box 3160, Long Beach, Calif. 90803.
James Dines & Co., Inc., Box 22, Belvedere, Calif. 94920.
Dow Theory Forecasts, Box 4550, Grand Central Station, New York 10017.
Dow Theory Letters, Inc. Box 1759, La Jolla, Calif. 92037.
Excelsior Research, Inc., 67 Wall Street, New York, N.Y. 10005.
The Forecaster, 19623 Ventura Boulevard, Tarzana, Calif. 91356.
Granville Market Letter, P.O. Box 58, Holly Hill, Fla. 32017.
The Holt Investment Advisory, 277 Park Avenue, New York, N.Y. 10017.
Indicator Digest, 451 Grand Avenue, Palisades Park, N.J. 07650.
Investors' Intelligence, 2 East Avenue, Larchmont, N.Y. 10602.
Key Volume Strategies, Box 407, White Plains, N.Y. 10602.
Lowry's Reports, 115 South 25th Road, Miami, Fla. 33129.
Merrill's Technical Trends, Box 228, Chappaqua, N.Y. 10514.
Powell Monetary Analyst, 63 Wall Street, New York, N.Y. 10005.
Professional Investor, Box 2144, Pompano Beach, Fla. 33061.
Slanker's International Investor's Viewpoint, 610 S.W. Alder, Portland, Ore. 97205.
Trendex Research Corp., 300 Maverick Bldg., San Antonio, Tex. 78205.
Wall Street Digest, 79 Wall Street, New York, N.Y. 10005.
Wall Street Irregular, Box 643B, New York, N.Y. 10021.
Worden & Worden, Inc., 1915 Floranada Road, Fort Lauderdale, Fla. 33308.
Zweig Forecast, 747 Third Avenue, New York, N.Y. 10017.

SOURCES OF INVESTMENT INFORMATION

Barron's, 22 Cortlandt Street, New York, N.Y. 10007.
The Chronicle, 110 Wall Street, New York, N.Y. 10005.
Finance, 8 West 40th Street, New York, N.Y. 10018.
Financial Weekly, P.O. Box 26565, Richmond, Va. 23261.
Financial World, 919 Third Avenue, New York, N.Y. 10022
Forbes, 70 Fifth Avenue, New York, N.Y. 10011.
Institutional Investor, 488 Madison Avenue, New York, N.Y. 10022.
Investment Dealers' Digest, 150 Broadway, New York, N.Y. 10038.
The Wall Street Journal, 22 Cortlandt Street, New York, N.Y. 10007.
Wall Street Transcript, 54 Wall Street, New York, N.Y. 10005.

Advance/Decline (A/D) lines, 2, 14, 16, 41, 84–86, 126
All-time highs, 54, 55
American Natural Resources Company, 44–45, 55
American Stock Exchange (AMEX), 16, 99, 141
American Telephone & Telegraph Company (AT&T), 21, 80, 126
Anaconda Company, 13
Anthony Industry, 119, 120
Appel, Gerard, 101–102
Applied Digital Data Systems, 84
Armstrong Cork Company, 43
Asarco, Inc., 143, 144
Ascending triangle chart pattern, 45, 46, 48
Associated Press, 113, 130
Austral Oil, 119
Averages:
    Group Stock, 113, 130
    [*See also* Dow Jones Industrial Average (DJIA); Dow Jones Transportation Average (DJTA); Dow Jones Utilities Average (DJUA); Moving average (MA)]
Averaging down, 157
Avon Products, 92, 126, 133

Bar charts, 24–26
Barron's, 69, 79, 80
    Confidence Index, 96–98
    Group Stock Averages, 113, 130
    Low-Priced Stock Index, 99
    10 High-Grade Bond Index, 111

Bear markets:
    characteristics of, 158
    in Dow Theory, 10–12
    in Elliott Wave Theory, 17, 18
    near-term overbought level in, 111
    selling short in (*see* Short selling)
    three-phase cycle of, 157, 159
    trend lines in, 31, 35
    volume and, 102
Bear trap, 51, 52
Best times to buy, 61–62
Bishop, G. W., Jr., 9, 10n.
Blackman, Richard, 31, 44, 70, 122–124
Block Activity Values (BAV), 143, 144
Blue Bell, Inc., 114–117
Bond stock yield differential, 111
Bottoms:
    market, 99
    stock, 32–33, 39–41, 157
Breakouts, 6, 54–57, 78
Brokerage firms, reporting of technical data by, 109–111
Bull markets:
    characteristics of, 158
    in Dow Theory, 11, 12
    in Elliott Wave Theory, 17, 18
    near-term overbought level in, 111
    short selling and, 133
    three-phase cycle of, 157, 158
    trend lines in, 30–31, 35
    volume and, 102
Bull trap, 51–52

Buy-and-hold policy, attitude of technician
    towards, 5, 13

Calls, 134, 141–146
Capital gains:
    attitude of technician towards, 5
    sell signals and, 123, 124
CD/QT (Cats and Dogs Versus Quality), 99
Channels, 71–72, 122–123
Chartcraft, Inc., 34, 35, 152
Charts, 2–6
    basic concept of, 21
    commodities futures trading and, 148–154
    false signals, 7
    finding declining stocks with, 130–132
    options and, 141, 143–144, 146
    patterns, 2, 11–12, 36–57
        breakouts, 6, 54–57, 78
        channels, 71–72, 122–123
        consolidation areas, 71, 77–78
        50% rule, 52–53, 158, 159
        flags and pennants, 48–49
        flat, 44–45
        gaps, 49–51
        Head & Shoulders (H&S), 42–44
        practice with, 57
        resistance levels, 71, 73–76, 110, 148
        saucer, 151, 152
        support levels, 71, 73–76, 110, 148
        traps, 51–52
        trend lines (see Trend lines)
        triangles, 45–48
        unfavorable, 53–54
        V formation, 37–41
        value of, 36
    plotting, 21–26
        Bar charts, 24–26
        Point and Figure (P&F), 21–24
    reading, 27–29
    sources of, 20–21
    statistical data used in (see Technical indicators)
    stop orders and, 136–138
    value of, 20
Chicago Board of Options Exchange (CBOE), 141
Commercial and Financial Chronicle, 79
Commodities futures trading, 18, 147–154
Composite Index, 101–102
Computerized premium returns, 146
Concepts on Profits in Commodity Futures
    Trading (Cox), 149
Confidence Index (CI), 96–98
Consolidation areas, 71, 77–78
Cover-loss price, 133
Covered call, 142
Cox, Houston A., Jr., 17, 149–151
Credit balances with brokers as technical
    indicator, 63–64
Crown Cork & Seal Company, Inc., 5

Day, best times to buy during, 62
Declining stock, guidelines for selling, 125–126
DeLutis, Donald C., 65–66
Descending triangle chart pattern, 45–48

Dines, James, 20
Discipline, 155
Discount-rate changes, 107–108, 126
DJ Momentum Ratio, 111
DJIA (see Dow Jones Industrial Average)
DJTA (see Dow Jones Transportation Average)
DJUA (see Dow Jones Utilities Average)
Double Tops and Bottoms (V chart patterns), 40–
    41
Dow, Charles H., 9
Dow, Jones & Company, Inc., 9
Dow Averages, 3, 12
    calculation of, 12
    criticisms of, 12–13
    use of, 15–17
    [See also Dow Jones Industrial Average (DJIA);
        Dow Jones Transportation Average
        (DJTA); Dow Jones Utilities Average
        (DJUA)]
Dow Chemical, 33, 34, 54–56, 75
Dow Jones Industrial Average (DJIA), 3, 12, 19
    accuracy of, 16
    Advance/Decline line compared to, 86, 126
    in bear market, 159
    in bull market, 158
    calculation of, 12, 16
    confirmation of trends with, 10
    defined, 12
    discount-rate changes and, 108
    50% rule and, 53
    fluctuations of, 1929–1976, 16
    London Financial Times Index forecasts of, 70
    moving averages and, 88–89, 93
    price/earnings multiple of, 109–110
    S&P's 500 compared to, 17
    sell signals and, 122–123
    short selling and, 66, 130, 132
    signs of market top and, 98
    summer rally, 61
    30-point week, 157
    year-end rally, 60
Dow Jones Transportation Average (DJTA), 3, 12
    calculation of, 12
    confirmation of trends with, 10
    criticisms of, 13
    defined, 12
Dow Jones Utilities Average (DJUA), 3, 12, 63
Dow Theory, 3, 9–15, 31
    basic concepts, 9–10
    interpretation, 10–12
    statistical data used in (see Dow Averages)
Downside breakouts, 57
Downtrend lines, 30, 31

Elliott, R. N., 18
Elliott Wave Theory, 17–19
Exxon Corporation, 80

Fan-Line Variation, 149, 150
Federal indicator, 108
Federal Reserve Board (FRB) reports, 105–108,
    126
50% rule, 52–53, 158, 159

Financial pages, 79–87
  Advance/Decline line, 2, 14, 16, 41, 84–86, 126
  Highs and Lows, 2, 86–87, 130
  Most Active stocks, 79–84, 113, 126, 130, 157
Financial Weekly, The, 79, 80, 99–101
Five-days action, 59
Five-week advance/decline diffusion index, 110
Flag chart pattern, 48, 49
Flat chart pattern, 44–45
Follow the Leaders (Blackman), 122–124
Forecasting indicators (*see* Technical indicators)
Fundamental analysis, 1
  basic approach of, 3–4
  versus technical analysis, 3–4, 56–57
  timing of selling and, 121–122

Gaines, Edythe, 64
Gaps in chart patterns, 49–51
General Electric Company, 13
General Motors Corporation (GM), 33, 34, 80, 126, 158, 159
Gould, Edson, Three Step-and-Stumble Rule of, 107–108
Graham, Benjamin, 7
Granville, Joseph E., 94, 102, 103, 122, 159, 160
Greiner, Perry P., 11*n*.
Group Stock Averages, 113, 130
Gulf & Western Industries, 21

Hamilton, W. P., 9
Head & Shoulders (H&S) chart pattern, 42–44
Highs and Lows, 2, 86–87, 130
Hirsch, Yale, 59
Historical patterns, 116–118, 131–132

IBM Corporation, 13, 126
Indicator Digest, 17, 96
Interest rates, 64–68
  discount-rate changes, 107–108, 126
  short interest, 67–68, 134, 158, 159
International Telephone & Telegraph Corporation (ITT), 81–82, 88
Inverted triangle chart pattern, 45, 47, 48
Investment performance, moving averages and, 90–92

January forecast, 59, 60
Jiler, William L., 45–48, 51, 52, 72, 73, 75
Johnson & Johnson, 53, 54

Keynes, John Maynard, 4
Krow, Harvey A., 85

Left Shoulder of Head & Shoulders (H&S) chart, 42, 43
Libbey-Owens-Ford Company, 77
Line, formation of, 10
Logarithmic paper, 24–25
London Financial Times Index, 69–70

Long-term chart, 114
Long-term trends, 34
Losses:
  attitude of technician towards, 5
  selling at, 125–127, 156
Low-Priced Stock Index, 99

Magee, John, 39, 41, 46, 49, 76
Margin requirement changes, Federal Reserve Board and, 107–108
Market bottom, 99
Market top, 98, 99
Member bank reserve changes (Federal Reserve Board report), 106
Merrill, Arthur A., 62
Merrill Lynch Round Lot Short Sale Ratio, 111
Midwest Stock Exchange, 141
Milgo Electronics, 83
Minnesota Mining & Manufacturing Company, 13
Monetary and reserve aggregates (Federal Reserve Board report), 106
Month, best times to buy during, 62
Most Active Moving Average (MA), 81
Most Active Moving Average Index, 80–81
Most Active stocks, 79–84, 113, 126, 130, 157
Moving average (MA), 2, 88–94
  commodities futures trading and, 151
  as criterion in setting trailing stops, 136, 137
  defined, 88
  five-week advance/decline diffusion index, 110
  Most Active Average Index, 80–81
  short-term trading guide and, 95–96
  200-Day, 92–94, 126
  uses of, 89–92
Mutual fund liquidity as technical indicator, 63

Naked calls, 142
National Semiconductor Corporation, 137–138
Neckline of Head & Shoulders (H&S) chart, 42–44
New York Magazine, 40
New York Stock Exchange, 16, 67, 69, 80, 89, 113, 141
  Common Stock Index, 17
  comparing AMEX indices to, 99
New York Times, The, 89

Odd Lot Short Sales Ratio (OLSSR), 68–69, 158, 159
Options, 141–146
Over-the-Counter (OTC) market, 16, 98

Pacific Exchange, 141
Patience, 156
Pennant chart pattern, 48–49
Percent of shares outstanding, 100
Philadelphia Exchange, 141
Point and Figure (P&F) charts:
  of commodities, 152–154
  plotting, 21–24
  trend lines on, 34–35

Polaroid Corporation, 37, 131
Post-Labor Day rally, 59–60
Premium, 142, 145, 146
Price versus market tables, 100–101
Price/earnings (P/E) ratio, 109–110, 114, 115
Price reversals, 23
Primary movement of stock market, 9–11
Probable Options Value, 143, 144
Professional Tape Reader, The, 33, 68, 119, 120, 136
Pullbacks, 154
Puts, 141
Pyramiding, 151–152

Quarter, best times to buy during, 61–62

Realism, 156
Relative Strength (RS), 118–120
Reserve requirement changes, Federal Reserve Board and, 107–108
Resistance levels, 71, 73–76, 110, 148
Reynolds Securities, Inc., 145, 146
Rhea, Robert, 9–11
Right Shoulder of Head & Shoulders (H&S) chart, 42–44

Saucer chart pattern, 151, 152
Schulz, John, 22, 23
Searle (G. D.) & Company, 46, 47
Seasonal forecasters, 59–61
Secondary movement of stock market, 9–11
Secondary offerings, 158, 159
Securities Research Company, Inc., 25, 32, 38, 45, 55, 69, 82, 83, 118, 131, 138
Selling:
  breakouts and, 56
  short (see Short selling)
  stop orders, 135–140, 156
  timing of, 121–127, 160
Shares outstanding, percent of, 100
Short interest, 67–68, 134, 158, 159
Short Interest Ratio (SIR), 67–68
Short selling, 128–134
  finding stocks, 130–132
  Merrill Lynch Round Lot Ratio, 111
  Most Active stocks and, 82
  rules for, 132–134
  Specialist Ratio, 69, 111
  stop orders for, 137–139
  as technical indicator, 66–69
  techniques of, 129
  using technical indicators for, 129–130
  V chart patterns and, 37–39
Short-term trading guide, 95–96
Sideways trend line, 31
Skyline Corporation, 136–137
Smart Money, 98
Specialist Short Selling Ratio (SSSR), 69, 111
Speculation Index, 99
Speculation indices, 99
Speculative Group Activity (SGA), 95–96

Standard & Poor's Composite Index of 500 Stocks, 15–17, 19
  DJIA compared to, 17
  sell signals and, 122
Standard & Poor's Index of 20 Low-Priced Common Stocks, 99
Standard & Poor's Stock Guide, 113
Stock market averages, using, 15–17
Stock market lore, 157, 160
Stock market theories, 9–19
  Dow Theory (see Dow Theory)
  Elliott Wave Theory, 17–19
Stock splits, 158, 159
Stop-limit orders, 135, 139–140
Stop loss, 135
Stop orders, 135–140, 156
Strategy of Daily Stock Market Timing for Maximum Profits, 159, 160
Strike price, 141, 142
Summer rally, 59, 61
Support levels, 71, 73–76, 110, 148
Symmetrical chart pattern, 45, 46, 48

Tandy Corporation, 32–34, 71–72, 123
Technical analysis, 1–8
  advantages of, 1, 2, 7
  basic approach of, 2
  characteristics of, 4–6
  focus of, 4
  versus fundamental analysis, 3–4, 56–57
  history of, 3
  indicators (see Technical indicators)
  negatives of, 6–7
  rules for, 155–157
  timing of selling and, 121–127
Technical indicators, 4–7, 58–70
  best times to buy, 61–62
  charts and (see Charts)
  commodities futures trading and, 148–154
  Composite Index, 101–102
  Confidence Index, 96–98
  credit balance with brokers, 63–64
  Federal Reserve Board reports and, 105–108, 126
  in financial pages (see Financial pages)
  interest rates (see Interest rates)
  London Financial Times Index, 69–70
  moving average [see Moving average (MA)]
  mutual fund liquidity, 63
  negatives of, 7
  percent of shares outstanding, 100
  price versus market, 100–101
  seasonal forecasters, 59–61
  short sales as, 66–69
  short selling and, 129–130
  short-term trading guide, 95–96
  signs of market top, 98–99
  speculation indices, 99
  timing of selling and, 121–127, 160
  utility stocks, 62–63
  velocity, 103–104
  volume, 5, 102–103, 126, 148–149
10 High-Grade Bond Index, 111
Texaco, Inc., 65

Three-Step-and-Stumble Rule, 107–108
Timing of selling, 121–127, 160
Tops:
   market, 98, 99
   stock, 39–41
Trailing stop order, 136–137
Traps, 51–52
Trend lines, 30–35
   of commodities, 149–152
   as criterion in setting trailing stops, 136, 137
   interpretation of, 30–34
   long-term trends, 34
   variations of, 34–35
   (*See also* Charts, patterns)
Trend reversals, 23
Trendline, Inc., 14, 28, 41, 43, 47, 50, 53, 64, 92,
    93, 97, 114, 115, 117
Trends, 2–3, 13, 20
   (*See also* Charts; Trend lines)
Triangular chart patterns, 45–48
200-Day Moving Average Ratio, 92–94, 126
Tyco Labs, 119

Upside breakouts, 54–57
Uptick, 129
Uptrending, 30, 31
Utility stocks as technical indicator, 62–63

V chart pattern, 37–41
Value Line, 17
Velocity analysis, 103–104
Volume analysis, 5, 102–103, 126, 148–149

W chart pattern, 40–41
Wall Street Journal, The, 3, 69, 79, 89
Ward, Kenneth, 3
Warner Communications, Inc., 49–50
Week, best times to buy during, 62
Weekly charts, 113
Weekly stock market tables, 113
Weinstein, Stan, 68*n*.
Winning stocks, selection of, 112–120
   historical pattern, 116–118
   Relative Strength (RS) approach, 118–120
   steps in, 113–116
Worden & Worden, 143*n*., 144
Wright Investors' Service, 91

Year-end rally, 60

Zero-plus tick, 129
Zweig, Martin E., 63–64, 108